THE
WAY OF
THE RABBI

Stories of Discipleship
from the Gospel of Mark

JIM SCHIRMER

a. Acorn
Press

Published by Acorn Press
An imprint of Bible Society Australia
ACN 148 058 306 | Charity licence 19 000 528
GPO Box 4161
Sydney NSW 2001
Australia
www.acornpress.net.au | www.biblesociety.org.au

ISBN 978-0-647-53346-8

First published by Morning Star Publishing in 2019,
ISBN 978-0-648-45373-4

A catalogue record for this book is available from the National Library of Australia

Cover and text design and layout by John Healy

Contents

Before there was a religion,

Before there were denominations,

Before any books had been published,

Before any songs had been written,

Before the chapels, churches and cathedrals,

Before the confessions,

Before the creeds,

Before the ceremonies,

Before councils and conferences and controversies,

Even before they were first called 'Christians':

Those who trusted their life to Jesus

Were known as followers of The Way.

Prologue

Featuring ...

A new game of an old name

The rues of rule books

Mark, his words

An answer to the question most asked

A new game of an old name

Can you play a game with me?

Imagine, for a moment, a different time. Imagine two people sitting together centuries, even millennia, in the future.

They know each other. They are both historians, working in the same library. And today they are seated together because they have been asked to analyse a new-found document that is hundreds of years old.

The document is about a game that has long died out and been forgotten. The paper is brittle and damaged. The language is obscure, so reading it is nearly impossible – even though they are adept at ancient languages. They can decipher a few words here and there: *bat... stump... run... in... catch... crease... eleven... pitch... over... out.*

And, after a while, they discern that the name of this mysterious game is ... *cricket*.

They look up at each other, with gaping mouths and eyes dry from painstaking reading, yet unblinking from wonder. But even without words, both of them know what has happened: they've made their discovery. A game so old that to them it is new.

Yet just as quickly as it came, the joy dissipates into a dilemma. What can they tell people? Indeed, what do they even know themselves? Above all else, will anyone care?

Now, I know full well that many people think the game of cricket is incomprehensible, even though it is still played in our times. But you can still imagine the exponential difficulty of reconstructing an entire game from just a few words, with their meaning further blurred by squinting through the thick lens of time.

Let's add to that dilemma that those historians, sitting in that future time, do not just want to understand the game of cricket, but they actually want to play the game. To do this, they would need to work out whether *bat* referred to a particular piece of equipment, or to something we do with our eyelids, or to a nocturnal flying mammal. They would need to discern whether *stump* is the bottom of a tree, or asking someone a question they can't answer, or something else entirely. Are *pitch* and *crease* verbs or nouns? *In* where? *Eleven* of what?

If you can feel the dilemma of these historians – eager amazement yet blinding confusion – I want you to consider this: Is this dilemma familiar?

Just think. For all of us who seek to live as disciples of the Rabbi Jesus, two thousand years since he last ate a meal on this earth, we are forced to live with this dilemma. Every day we are meant to believe, trust and even live out a whole lexicon of words that are just as ancient and unfamiliar as the words of cricket were to those two future historians. *Worship, salvation, faith, mission, holiness, redemption, evangelism, repentance.* They all mean something, no doubt about it. But when was the last time you heard these words in everyday conversation? If you used them with your neighbours, would they understand you? Would they care? And, most importantly, would they know how to 'play'?

But there is more. There is the word that is possibly the most confusing of all: the name of the game itself. It occurs more times in the gospels than any of the other words mentioned, because it was the game that Jesus himself spent the most time playing: *disciple.*

Though you may think you know it well, this is a word that is remarkably foreign to us. A word so rarely heard in everyday conversation that it practically means nothing to the average woman or man. Yet it is a word so strikingly close to the heart of the ministry of Jesus the Nazarene that it is impossible to understand him, the movement he founded or even ourselves without it.

For us to understand this word in our world, we will have to work for our meal. We will have to stare hard at ancient words, while also imagining the game unfolding. This is the reason for this book: to engage with the story of Jesus and his disciples and, by reading his story, to imagine the Way of the Rabbi in our times.

So I invite you on this journey of remembering and imagining. Walk with me upon Galilean sand, witness conflicts and miracles, and be astounded and puzzled at the same time. As we read this story, I wonder whether maybe, just maybe, you might hear a voice in your ears that is neither mine nor yours, faintly calling through the years and echoing through the centuries:

'Come, follow me.'

I wonder what might happen, to your world and to our world, if we did.

The rues of rule books

To understand the next step, let us go back to our historians, leaning over the book about the strange game of cricket:

They manage to decipher more and more of their mysterious document. They soon discover that what they are translating is a text named *The Laws of Cricket*.[1]

Word by word, then line by line, they start to learn more and more about the strange words.

From Law 1.1 they learn 'A match is to be played between two sides, each of eleven players'.

Later, they learn in Law 6.1 that the bat 'consists of two parts, a handle and a blade' and 'One end of the handle is inserted into a recess in the blade as a means of joining the handle and the blade' (Law 6.3a).

The pitch

… is a rectangular area of the ground 22 yards/20.12 m in length and 10 ft/3.05 m in width. It is bounded at either end by the bowling creases and on either side by imaginary lines, one each side of the imaginary line joining the centres of the two middle stumps, each parallel to it and 5 ft/1.52 m from it. (Law 7.1)

On and on it goes. Law by law, line by line, clauses and subclauses, certainties and exceptions. Explaining everything from innings to intervals, from when the wicket is down to when the wicket is kept, from lost balls to dead balls to wide balls and even no balls. Each word precise. Each sentence exact. No loopholes. No misunderstandings. After all, it is a book of laws, and laws have no tolerance for ambivalence.

Still, for all they achieve, laws do not have a priority for praxis. It is their job to define, delineate and stipulate. This is their purpose, but also their limitation. Prescribing is different from playing. To read the laws

---

[1] All quotes taken from Marylebone Cricket Club, *The Laws of Cricket* (2000 Code 5th Edition, 2013), https://www.lords.org/mcc/laws-of-cricket/.

of the game is different from playing the game, inasmuch as knowing that the physics formula for momentum is different from being hit by a speeding truck.

You have probably encountered a similar difficulty if you have ever tried to explain a new game to someone (whether that is a sport, party game, a board game or card game or any other type of game). Explaining the rules only takes you so far. The rules give the parameters of the game – just enough knowledge to get started – but soon enough you will have to say, 'Let's just give it a go', 'Watch me for a round, and then join in' or 'Let's have a practise and see if you have any questions'.

The same can be said about the pursuit of discipleship. Following the Way of Jesus cannot be reduced to watertight rules.

I should know – I've tried.

From as early as I could remember, I have been surrounded by people who sincerely centred their lives around the question of how it would look to live like Jesus in their own unique context. I was fascinated by these devoted disciples – most of whom were members of my own family – and in adult life I could think of no better calling than to devote myself to this very same question.

My story started in a regulation way: ministering in church communities, teaching in Bible colleges and studying in seminaries. Strangely enough, it was my theological training that started me asking questions. It is difficult to study the life of Jesus so intently without starting to feel some incongruence between his life and the organised religion that continues in his name.

That dissonance grew to the point of discomfort, at which point my family and I left traditional church ministry to pursue a call to serve people at the margins of church and society. Where I had been running youth groups on Friday nights, I was now playing soccer with refugee children; where I had been a preacher spruiking salvation, I was now a counsellor listening to stories of survival; where I had been coordinating ministries from offices, I was now mentoring faith in homes.

What never changed, however, was my obsession with the question: what does it mean to imitate Jesus in one's unique, individual life? I turned from one rule book to the next to see if they could teach me the game. I read book after book after book. Nearly all were helpful; many were wise, and some were sublime. As I write this, I still have these books on a shelf just to the left of where I sit; many are dog-eared for quick reference.

Yet for all that they gave me, these books could no more teach me the game of discipleship than a rule book could. I needed something else. I needed an example. An experience.

A story.

And one day I discovered what I needed. I discovered a story of someone playing the game. In fact, the story of the master of the game. It was like the stick figure sketches that I had been staring at had suddenly grown flesh and leapt from the page into my room to play the game in front of my eyes. It would be like the future historians, translating *The Laws of Cricket*, suddenly discovering a film of a master the sport. If they could watch Don Bradman strike the ball, they would know what the bat was for and what it could do.

And as soon as I read it, I wondered why I had spent so long reading the rule books when I could have been reading the gospels.

Mark, his words

*Each gospel was written to proclaim the good news about Jesus Christ.
But Jesus is never a solitary figure.*

—Francis J. Moloney[2]

One of the simplest and yet most meaningful definitions of a story that I have ever heard defines a story as 'events linked in sequence across time according to a plot'.[3]

Arguably, in that definition of a story, the final word is the most influential. The other elements – the events, the sequence and the timing – are all easily seen but it is actually the plot that steers the direction of all three. Yet it is not so obvious. It is the hidden influence, the rudder for the ship.

Invisible though it may be, it is possible to trace the influence of the plot by looking at its effects on the more visible elements of the story. In this way, you might follow the sequence of images in a tapestry or carving to understand the narrative it depicts. You may notice the themes that are repeated in various episodes of a TV serial. You can witness it in the cause and effect storyline of a video game. And, of course, you can sense it developing through the pages of a good book, so that when you get to the end and someone asks you, 'What was it about?' you can answer without having to repeat every word that you read.

The theme (or themes) of a story are the 'red threads' that run from beginning to end. The image of a red thread comes from the British Royal Navy, perhaps the most dominant ocean-going force of history. Every rope on every ship of the British Navy is marked in a special way. Within all the cords woven together, there is always a single red thread that winds its way through. No matter where you cut the rope,

---

2 Francis J. Moloney, *Mark: Storyteller, Interpreter, Evangelist* (Peabody: Hendrickson Publishers, 2004), 159.
3 This comes from the fascinating and rich world of Narrative Therapy. Alice Morgan, *What is narrative therapy? An easy-to-read introduction* (Adelaide: Dulwich Centre, 2000), 129–130.

you can always see the red thread and know that this is a rope of the navy. Furthermore, if you got a hold of the thread you could follow it through the entire length of the rope, through every twist, knot or tear, right the way to the end.

So if we accept that we need to re-imagine discipleship in the way of Jesus, and if we understand that we need a story, not just a rule book, to play the game, then this book is organised around meeting this goal through a single objective: to discover and follow the story-thread of discipleship through the narrative of Jesus' life as recorded by the writer known as Mark.

By doing this, I am certainly not saying that this is the only thread that you can follow through Mark's version of the good news. I don't think I would even dare to say that this is the most important. Like all of the gospels, Mark records the story of the culmination of the mission of Israel, of Jesus coming to fulfil the mission of the God of Israel, of the beginning of a new community covenanted to this God, and of the clash of this kingdom against the other powers of the world.[4] In this way, there are many enriching and moving threads that we could follow: the unfolding revelation of Jesus' identity; the arm wrestle with the powers of evil; the steady journey towards the moment of passionate sacrifice; or the invasion of God's kingship into the world.

Interwoven with each of these soaring themes runs another thread: the story of how Jesus calls, knows, sends, leads and eventually upends a group of disciples. It is like a red thread through the story; like a gentle, steady movement gliding underneath the crescendo of a symphony.

To this end, this book is a reading of the Gospel of Mark that highlights, prioritises and emphasises the Story of Discipleship. We will follow this thread from the beginning of the gospel to the end, word by word and scene by scene. This book is designed to be read with a

---

4 For a powerful overview of the key themes of the gospel narratives see Tom Wright, *How God became King* (London: SPCK, 2012).

copy of Mark's gospel close at hand in order to read the stories yourself as we reflect on them together.

Yet the ultimate goal is not to create another rule book. The gift of story is that it favours imagination over instruction. Rather than giving directions to follow, the story leaves us with questions to answer in our own lives – questions that might enable us to envisage what the Way of the Rabbi could look like if we took up this apprenticeship here and now. After all, what good is understanding a game if we never give it a try?

An answer to the question most asked

My father lived in a time of educational cruelty. His senior years of school involved spending two years of classes in which he and his peers were meant to memorise every part of the curriculum. Then, at the end of those two years, each subject was assessed by sitting a single, epic exam. Two years of work all at stake in a couple of hours.

When he sat his German exam, he had to read and answer comprehension questions about a passage. This particular passage was about *kuhschwanz*. If you, like me, cannot speak German, this word means 'cow's tail'. Unfortunately, for my father, he did not know this word either. But because the word was so critical, so central to the passage, the fact that he could not understand it made the passage practically incomprehensible.

Can you imagine reading line after line, trying to guess what this was all about, and worse, answering questions about what it was all about? I have nightmares about situations like this. He was living it.

Needless to say, he has never forgotten the meaning of the word *kuhschwanz*. As his son, I like to think that the last words on his lips will be the names of loved ones, however, sometimes I wonder whether he will go to his death whispering '*kuhschwanz*'.

This is why I need to answer the question I get asked most often: What is a disciple?

If we are going to spend so much time talking about it, we need to understand what it means. Otherwise, the story that follows will be like a foreign language.

The simplest and most literal translation of the word 'disciple' would be the word 'learner'.[5] However, this needs further clarification because often we would use the word 'student' as a synonym for the

---

5 W.E. Vine, Merrill F. Unger & William White (eds.), *An Expository Dictionary of Biblical Words* (Nashville: Thomas Nelson, 1984), 171ff.

word 'learner'. In our culture, the word 'student' comes with the image of a child, young person or young adult sitting at a desk at school or in a lecture at university. But this is not the way a disciple learnt in the time of Jesus. A disciple was not just a student. A disciple was also an adherent to the teacher. A disciple's job was not just to listen but also to imitate.

Luckily, we have a modern-day equivalent word that does a lot better job of describing a disciple than the words 'student' or 'learner'. The better way of describing a disciple would be as an 'apprentice'. The distinction is this: an apprentice learns through an active and reflective process in which they learn to do the job that their master already knows how to do.[6]

In other words, an apprentice is learning how to do the job of their master. If someone is doing an apprenticeship in mechanics, they are learning how to be a mechanic from a mechanic. It therefore goes without saying that this requires a special relationship and a special method. The master is an example as much as he or she is a lecturer. Learning happens along the way, as techniques are shown and mistakes are corrected. Practise is as important as recital.

Therefore, a disciple of Jesus = an apprentice of Jesus.

The other term that is often used to translate the word disciple is the word 'follower'. This, too, carries a particular image. For instance, one rabbi once instructed his disciples that they must 'Bathe in the dust of [their] rabbi's feet'.[7] As Rob Bell writes:

This idea of being covered in the dust of your rabbi comes from something everybody had seen. A rabbi would come to town, and right behind him would be this group of students, doing their best to keep up with the rabbi as he went about teaching his yoke from one place to another. By the end of a day of walking in the dirt directly behind their

---

[6] In other disciplines, there are other similar words. If you come from the field of drama or music or dance, you could use the word 'understudy'. Or if you are from a long, long time ago, in a galaxy far, far away, you could say 'Padawan'.
[7] Mishnah, Seder Nezikin, Tractate Avot, 1:4.

rabbi, the students would have the dust from his feet all over them.[8]

For better or for worse, we also have a modern-day equivalent of this. We, too, 'follow' people, but more often in the world of Twitter. If you become a follower of someone on Twitter, you are basically saying the same thing that a disciple says to a rabbi: 'Your every thought, word and action is so important to me that I do not want to miss a single thing you think, say or do'.

Therefore, a disciple of Jesus = a follower of Jesus.

Combining these words, we will assume that to be a disciple means being an apprentice-follower of Jesus. But, as I lamented before, just having a definition is like trying to master a game just by reading the rule book.

We need to start telling the story. For the sake of our church and our world, we need to start telling it urgently.

---

8 Rob Bell, *Velvet Elvis* (Grand Rapids: Zondervan, 2005), 130.

The Story of the Call

Mark 1:1–2:17

Featuring ...

Backdrop: the secret call of Rabbi Jesus

Why were they fishermen?

When two contagious humans touch

Hospitals for the healthy

The way today: vocation

The way today: 3

Finding our way: the first and second questions

Backdrop: the secret call of Rabbi Jesus

Mark 1:1–15

In the world of storytelling, there is a principle known as 'Chekov's Gun', created by the Russian playwright of the same name. Paraphrased roughly, it reads something like this: if there is a gun on the table at the start of the book, it better be fired by the time the book ends.

In other words, any good storyteller knows that it is crucial to begin a story with the end in mind. The establishing shot of a film, the journalist's lead sentence and the opening bars of an opera – the storyteller has one objective. The storyteller must set the scene for the action that is about to ensue, and the reader expects her to do so. Hence, if we find a gun on the table at the start of the book, we expect it to be fired later on.

Many of the great stories – and also many of the not so great ones – do this with a prologue. As a child, I thought that 'prologue' must have been some ancient word for 'optional', because I often skipped over this short bit of text that just didn't seem to have anything to do with the 'real' story.

This was a mistake, of course, for the prologue is written to contain critical backstory; without it the reader would be lost. For the reader, it is a small parcel of knowledge, neatly gift-wrapped, and sometimes obscure but nonetheless important. Sometimes the knowledge that the reader has is a secret to everyone else in the story.

Mark's version of the good announcement of Jesus begins in the same way. The story does not begin with a baby in Bethlehem, angels on high or even 'in the beginning'. We land in the middle, on a dusty desert road leading to the Jordan River, with a wild prophet preaching renewal, saying that he is paving the road for God's anointed king. It is here that we learn the knowledge that will carry us through the story: that Jesus from Nazareth is the anointed child of God. He will bring near the reign of God, and he will oppose any force that dehumanises or destroys God's creation.[1]

Read the first page of the Gospel of Mark and you will know at least this much. You know it, I know it, Jesus knows it. But everyone else in the story needs to figure it out. It's a secret at this stage and the grand story of Mark is about how this secret comes to light. It is like he is writing a murder mystery. The reader sees who commits the murder in the first chapter, and then they watch as every other character in the story uncovers what the reader already knows. Some characters move closer to the truth, while others seem to move further away. But I will say no more on that at this stage – I hate spoilers and I imagine that you do too.

From a storyteller's point of view, what happens next is perhaps just as important. After the prologue comes chapter one. Even novice writers know to quickly introduce main characters and themes.

Christopher Vogler, the great teacher of storytelling (whose writings have inspired some of the most memorable films and books from the last few decades), describes the crucial significance of a main character's first appearance:

> [The] most important [thing] is: What is the character *doing* at the moment of entrance? The character's first action is a wonderful opportunity to speak volumes about his attitude, emotional state, background, strengths, and problems. The first action should be a model of the hero's characteristic attitude and the future problems or solutions that will result. The first behaviour we see should be characteristic. It should define and reveal character.[2]

Therefore, we should truly recognise just how significant it is that the first thing Jesus does in his ministry is to gather a group of disciples. It is as significant as Frodo Baggins leaving the Shire with dangerous magic in his pocket; young Harry Potter getting mysterious letters delivered by an owl; Dorothy taking her dog Toto and running away

---

1 John Smith, *Advance Australia Where?* (Australia: ANZEA, 1989), 188.
2 Christopher Vogler, *The Writer's Journey* (3rd ed.) (Chelsea: Sheridan Books, 2007), 89.

from home, or Jim Hawkins happening upon a map to buried treasure and following its course.

Think about it! Jesus could not hesitate for even a day before he did this. There was nothing in his mind – not teaching, healing, worshipping or anything else – that was more important than discipleship. That was his priority, his number one, the top of his to-do list – his first step in bringing God's kingdom on earth.

As the study of human communication has so clearly established, the medium is the message. By choosing, using and *prizing* apprenticeship as the medium of establishing God's kingdom, Jesus is sending a clear message. This kingdom is not going to be won by those who fought – that is the way of politics. This kingdom is not a product that can be bought – that is the way of the market. This kingdom is not a doctrine that can be taught – that is the way of religion.

No, instead this kingdom is a spirit that needs to be caught – that is the way of the Rabbi. That is the way of love.

Why were they fishermen?

Mark 1:16–20

Why were they fishermen?

Or, more importantly, why does Mark bother to tell us that they were fishermen? He has already commented that Jesus was by a lake and that these men were out on the lake casting their net into the water. Then he adds, 'because they were fishermen'. I'm not sure why else they would be casting a fishing net into the lake unless they were fishermen, but Mark felt the need to add the redundant detail anyway.

When details are redundant, yet included, they are often important. So, why were they fishermen?

There are two answers. Strangely enough, both are true.

Answer 1

To understand this answer, we first need to get a sense of the educational system of the time. The Mishnah (the first major written collection of Jewish oral teaching about the Torah) sets it out as this:[3]

At age five, education would begin. It was called the age of Scripture. It was based on the Torah (what we know as the first five books of the Bible). By studying this, the students would learn to read and write in Hebrew and study the story, culture and customs of their people, as well as the religious commandments. It was a rounded education, much like primary school is today. It would also focus on memorising as much of the Torah as possible. The teacher, of course, was the town's local rabbi.

At around the age of 10, there was the first cut. We have no evidence to suggest that any girls went beyond this stage (if they were included at all in the first stage), and many boys would leave school to learn the family trade.

---

3 Mishnah, Seder Nezikin, Tractate Avot, 5:21–22

The rest – if they were good enough, that is – moved onto the equivalent of secondary school. This was called the age of Interpretation. Here, they read the other parts of the Scriptures – the prophets and the writings. They would also learn more advanced ways of thinking, such as how to interpret and apply the Scriptures in their lives. However, there was again an emphasis on repetition and memorisation. There were few accessible books and absolutely no search engines so, unlike modern education (which focuses on accessing readily available information), the methods focused on being able to remember things for a lifetime.

Around the age of 15, the remaining boys would go through another cut. Most – and I really do mean most – would go and learn their family's trade. A select few would continue study in the equivalent of tertiary education. This was called the age of Instruction. Having memorised the entire Old Testament, as well as having learnt skills in interpretation and application, they would then focus on some of the most prized skills of all: questioning, debate, commentary, rhetoric and communication.

If someone was still being educated in their late teens, they were destined for some sort of profession, not just a trade. They might be a scribe, a doctor or a lawyer. But a very, very few of those who started would go on to the highest calling of all.

At around the age of 20, the best and the brightest would be approached by their rabbi who would say, 'Come and follow me'. This was the age of Vocation. They would become the rabbi's disciples. They would bathe in his dust. For 10 years they would follow and learn until, at the age of 30, they would have the authority to become a rabbi themselves.

So why were Simon, Andrew, James and John fishermen?

In this system, it was because they weren't good enough to be disciples. Whether it was at age 10, 15 or 20, they had dropped out of the program. At some stage, someone (maybe even themselves) had said, 'You're not going to make it', 'You're not good enough', 'Go home'.

And so, they became fishermen. Why? Because they weren't good enough to be disciples.

Answer 2

In this context, the meaning of Jesus' invitation to follow him would have been unmistakable. Their reaction certainly indicates that they knew exactly what he meant. 'Come follow me' meant a call to the vocation of apprenticeship under a rabbi.

Yet these three words were not the only words Jesus spoke. When he called them to discipleship, he also announced that he would make them 'fishers of men'. And with these words, Jesus gave his own answer as to why they were fishermen.

So, while they were fishermen precisely because they were not good enough to be disciples, in Jesus' eyes, being fishermen was what made them good enough to be his disciples. He didn't need his disciples to be experts. He didn't need the best, the brightest, the most beautiful, the brainiest, the brawniest, the most bountiful, or the most blessed. His job was to cast his net over human beings and tangle them up in what he was doing. He needed disciples who knew how to do that. He needed fishermen.

So … why were they fishermen?

Because they weren't disciples.

But why did Jesus choose them as disciples?

Because they were fishermen.

This begs further questions: if Jesus walked into my life, where would he find me? What would I be doing? Why would I be doing it? What are my equivalents of 'the Sea of Galilee', 'casting nets' or 'being a fisherman'?

How might all of my places, activities and roles prove to be the workshop of my apprenticeship to Jesus?

When two contagious humans touch

Mark 1:21–45

Up until now, the story has been setting itself up, like a rollercoaster carriage steadily clicking upwards. Then, suddenly, it reaches its summit, its tipping point. There is the eternal moment of anticipation; the floating stillness between security and danger. Everything is about to become so fast that it will make everything before it seem ever so slow.

And then, the story tips.

Suddenly, Rabbi Jesus is on the move. Teaching. Persuading. Debating. The crowds sense his authority but only one man in the crowd senses that there is something more to him. Something in this man knows the secret about this rabbi and shrieks in fear. Jesus commands and the spirit flees. News spreads.

Immediately, Jesus goes into a home and heals Simon's mother-in-law. The whole town begins to gather at the house, bringing all their problems. Jesus responds. He heals them through the night, and in the early morning, he seeks some solitude. Even then, everyone is looking for him.

The word is out. The carriage cannot be stopped now. It is all speed – twists and turns, drops and loops and blurs of colour.

Then a man appears. People hear the man before they see him because the customs require him to wear a bell like an animal. He is sick – the infectious, untouchable type of sick. His nerves are dying. His body is marked with the leprosy. No one has brought him to Jesus because no one goes to the man at all. So far, all of the sick people they had brought were the good kind of sick, those you can touch and care for; those who have an opportunity for healing.

But for this man, he has to organise his own healing. He has to step out. He has to break the law to see the rabbi. But still he comes. He kneels.

He begs.

I've never had to beg. Have you? I think that either way, you can understand the humiliation.

Then, just as suddenly as the story sped up, the story slows down. The carriage comes to a halt. The writer takes pains to focus us in on Jesus' hand. It is so close that you can see the pores where the follicles join the skin. You can see the greenish-blue of the veins, and the sheen on his palm as it involuntarily moistens with fear at the thought of touching the infectious skin of the leper. The dust on his hand blends with the sweat, and the faint musk of wet earth is caught in the breeze.

The hand trembles slightly, but it reaches out slowly, until its skin is against the skin of the other. At that moment, every person in the crowd holds their breath. For in that moment, something happened.

Two contagious forces have touched.

In that brief, brief moment, no one knows which force will prevail. Will Jesus catch this man's disease, so hideous and so infectious? Or will this man catch Jesus' compassion, so captivating and so regenerating?

For a moment it all hangs in the balance.

The whole force of evil – illness, decay, isolation, condemnation, shame, fear, sorrow, hopelessness, death, fear. So much fear.

The whole presence of God – compassion, courage, mercy, healing, power, restoration, hope, comfort, acceptance, love, life.

Good and evil, skin to skin.

What happened when these two men touched is what happens at the heart of our souls. Our lives are a touching of these two contagious forces. Good and evil. Saint and sinner. Created and fallen.

I have no doubt that you know the place in your life that needs the touch of Jesus. If your life is like mine, you try to avoid this place or try to heal it by your own power. Either way, it becomes the leprosy of your life, hidden away in a cave lest its horror is seen by those around you.

This is the hour to come out of the cave, to come to the rabbi, to kneel and to beg. It is time to seek Jesus out in the place where you are wounded. This is the hour to pray like a leper would pray, daring that you will encounter compassion, rather than indifference. Trusting in the *empathy* of God. Trusting that Jesus' touch is contagious.

This is the hour to cry out, 'If you are willing!' and to hear, 'I *am* willing!'

Hospitals for the healthy

Mark 2:1–17

During World War II, there were some Jewish prisoners in the Nazi concentration camps who fared better than others. These prisoners were known as the *Capos* (sometimes spelled 'Kapo'). The Capos were chosen to carry out duties of supervision and administration, relieving the SS of such menial tasks. In return, the Capos were rewarded with securities and 'luxuries' (relatively speaking) that were not enjoyed by the common Jewish prisoner. The Capos assisted in the oppression of the common Jewish prisoner and were being rewarded for it.

We do not need much imagination to understand how the common prisoner felt about the Capos. In his timeless account, Victor Frankl explained what he and his fellow prisoners thought of these people:

> While these ordinary prisoners had little or nothing to eat, the Capos were never hungry; in fact many of the Capos fared better in the camp than they had in their entire lives. Often they were harder on the prisoners than were the guards, and beat them more cruelly than the SS men did. These Capos, of course, were chosen only from those prisoners whose characters promised to make them suitable for such procedures … they soon became much like the SS men and the camp wardens, and may be judged on a similar psychological basis.[4]

In the first century during the Roman occupation of Israel, there was a similar class of person. The Romans were efficient in violence, but their bureaucracy required more labour. They recruited local subjects to run their business and they rewarded them in a similar way as the Capos. Under this role they probably fared much better than they had in their entire lives.

So when we turn to the story of Jesus and we read of 'tax collectors and other sinners', we need to think like we are a Jewish prisoner looking at a well-fed Capo.

---

4 Victor E. Frankl, *Man's Search for Meaning* (London: Rider, 2004), 17–18.

'Follow me.'

These words are spoken again, this time to someone like a Capo –
even as he sat in his office, with his tools of oppression on his desk. Yet
even he could be a disciple. Even he was not beyond the rabbi's reach.
The rabbi just proved that he has the authority to forgive sins in the
same way he has the power to make a lame man walk.

The Story of the Call starts with Rabbi Jesus calling the disciples to
imagine what the world would be like if God was king.[5] So the story
continues with those who Jesus calls to be his apprentices in this craft.
Fisherman. Lepers. Capos. By calling the people he calls, Jesus draws a
line in the sand. This kingdom is not a school for the literate. It is not a
hospital for the healthy. It is not a temple for the righteous.

It is easy to say that Jesus' call is for everyone, yet implicitly what
this means is that it is for anyone. In calling who he did, Rabbi Jesus
made it clear that anyone, no matter who they were or what they did,
could join this apprenticeship.

---

[5] Such is the imagination of the prophets: Walter Brueggmann, *The Practice of Prophetic
Imagination* (Minneapolis: Fortress Press), 2.

The way today: vocation

So, what might it look like if the Story of the Call was written in our own lives?

The Latin word for 'call' is *voco*. In English we use this root in words like vocal, evoke and advocate. It is also the root of the word *vocation*.

Usually the way we use the word 'vocation' is to refer to someone's job, but for many it seems to be a very formal word for what we do day-to-day. For example, my first job was working stocking the shelves at a discount variety shop. You know the type, right? The type of shop with the ads that have someone shouting at you because the prices are just so cheap. The type of shop where everything is $2 and there are aisles of things you would never need, yet you can never find what you are looking for.

So, for three years I wheeled out boxes, cut them open and lined the shelves with everything that no one could possibly need. For 10 months of the year, I left home at 6.00am to start at 7.00am; in the two months before Christmas, I started at 10.00pm and worked through the night. I cleaned up vomit once or twice, rude customers shouted at me often and I once even helped to catch a shoplifter.

The job certainly didn't feel as fancy as a vocation. To me, a better word would be 'station'. It was where my carriage had pulled over and stopped for that part of my life. Believe me, I was certainly peering out the window, impatiently waiting for the train to start moving me into more exciting territory. From what I've learnt, I'm not the only one who has had this feeling about their station in life.

I had other stations in my life as well, of course. During the time I was working at this shop, I was also a youth worker and a student. I was a son, a brother, a roommate, a friend and a boyfriend. I was the tenant of a rental property and I was a neighbour. I was a resident and a citizen. From week to week, I would also find myself as a football watcher, a car driver, an internet user, a book reader and a multitude of other things. I'm sure you could come up with a list for yourself.

It gives some comfort to read Mark's Story of the Call and find ordinary people introduced according to their stations: fisher, leper, mother-in-law, teacher, sinner, or even something as humdrum as just a member of the crowd. So, given these oh-so-common stations, what can we learn from how Jesus calls them? What do we learn about a disciple's *vocation*?

To answer that question, we first need to reflect upon how we commonly conceptualise the life of a Christian. Then we compare that with what Jesus did in the gospels.

Arguably the most influential model of the stages of a Christian life is the Engel Scale (named after its key developer, James F. Engel).[6] While many are not familiar with the details of this model, the logic is remarkably close to what you've learnt in Christian teaching.

What Engel sought to do in constructing this scale was to describe a schema that was both universal (i.e. everyone is on it) and linear (i.e. each step follows the one before it). Engel proposed that the moment of conversion to Christian faith is like the number 0. Every step before conversion is seen as a series of negative numbers progressing towards knowledge and acceptance of the gospel towards the point of conversion. Every step after conversion is a positive number, signifying stages of growth and development in faith.

The Engel Scale is famous for its logic and pragmatism. The scale assumes that everyone is on it somewhere. You can test this by asking yourself, 'Which number currently describes where I am with my faith?' and you should be able to find an answer. It also has a practical application, as the job of ministry is to encourage individuals to step further along the journey.

---

6 First published in J.F. Engel & H.W. Norton, *What's Gone Wrong With the Harvest?* (Grand Rapids: Zondervan, 1975).

Basically, the Engel Scale – and the broader logic that it characterises – separates the Christian life into two halves which hinge on a single point: conversion. For people on the 'negative' side of conversion, we do 'evangelism' and for people on the 'positive' side we do 'discipleship'. Again, while you may have never heard of this scale before, you can probably hear echoes of it in the way we commonly discuss the Christian life or organise ministry in our church communities.

Yet when we read the Story of the Call, we see Jesus doing very little 'evangelism' as we know it. Instead, from the moment he meets people, he 'vocates' them into an apprenticeship. No matter where you are on the Engel Scale, no matter what station you have in your life, you have a calling, a vocation to follow Jesus and to learn his trade of restoring creation to how God intended it. Fishermen, lepers, tax collectors, mothers, fathers, children, sick, healthy, rich, poor, unemployed, single, married, the last, the least, the lost, the loser. This job is for everyone, and that means that it can be for anyone.

Yet as soon as we say this we are forced to consider: is this not itself good news? Is this vocation not gospel? If so, wasn't this Jesus doing evangelism? Sure – none of the people who accept Jesus' call have been 'converted' in the way we normally define it. Ask them their religion and they would say, 'We follow the God of Abraham, Isaac and Jacob, who revealed his name to Moses'. None of them proclaimed Jesus as Lord. They did not invite him into their heart or pray the sinner's prayer. None of them (that we know of from Mark's Gospel) had been baptised. On the Engel Scale, they would be in the negative numbers.

Yet … in the fisherman, the rejected ones are chosen. In the leper, the unclean one is restored. In the tax collector, the enemy is made a friend.

The same is true for us. Wherever we find ourselves parked in life, our stations become vocations. The place where we find ourselves becomes the workshop of our apprenticeship. Every task, role and relationship contains the potential for a lesson in how to be more like Jesus.

The Story of the Call teaches us that evangelism, conversion and discipleship are all one and the same: if we take up an apprenticeship to Jesus then our lives are being converted into his, each moment to the next. The vocation of discipleship redeems the ordinary, transforms the mundane and saves the everyday.

As I described before, when I worked in customer service at the discount retail store, I was deeply unhappy with my station. I wanted to follow Jesus in a more exciting way. I wanted preaching tours and revival rallies. Let's face it, I wanted my name remembered by those I wowed with wonders. But one day, as I opened another box, slapped another sticker on another item and placed it all on a shelf, I had a moment where I lived the Story of the Call:

One day, as the Spirit of Jesus moved through the aisles of the shop, he saw a young man pricing the stock and packing the shelves.

And the Spirit said, 'Come, follow me, and I will make you a servant not just of customers but of humankind'.

Stop what you are doing – stop right where you are. Close your eyes and open your ears. Listen. Listen. What might Jesus be calling out to you?

The way today: 3

One of the oldest stories that has survived to us is the epic of Homer's *Odyssey*, the story of Odysseus' long journey home after the Trojan War. In spite of its name, the story does not start with Odysseus. It begins with his son Telemachus, in a crisis, defending the estate of his father (who is presumed dead) and protecting his mother from a horde of suitors. Telemachus is faced with an impossible choice: stay and defend or head out onto the sea to seek his father.

Telemachus has few allies, but one that he does have is an old friend of his father's: the wise and faithful Mentor. Mentor counsels, supports and advocates for Telemachus.

At one point early in the story, we find Telemachus in the midst of his dilemma, and in his desperation, he lifts his hands up in prayer to the goddess Athene:

> Hear, I beg you! It was your command that I should sail across the misty seas to find out whether my long-lost father is ever coming back. But my countrymen, and above all those suitors that besiege my mother, are thwarting me at every point.[7]

This was his prayer, and the goddess Athene chose to answer it. But, like the Greek gods often do, she chose a disguise with which to speak to him.

> Athene drew near to him, and *assuming the form and voice of Mentor*, addressed him with winged words.[8]

For me, this is perhaps one of the most insightful images in all of literature. When the divine wishes to speak to the mortal, this is done in the form and voice of another mortal. Of course, whether we have realised it or not, every time we use the word 'mentor', we are referring back to this character's name in Homer's *Odyssey*. What was just a name to Homer has become its own word in English to describe one

---

7 Homer, *The Odyssey* (London: Penguin Classics, 2003), 21–22.
8 Homer, *The Odyssey* (London: Penguin Classics, 2003), 21–22. Emphasis added.

of the most distinct and profound types of relationship in human experience. Anyone who has had the presence of a mentor in their life would resonate with this: the gift of a mentor is a touch of the divine.

This image is essential for us as apprentices of Jesus. To this point in the application of the story, we have largely dealt with the ethereal. The mere idea of transforming to be more and more like Jesus is compelling enough that it might distract us from the practical, pragmatic questions of how this will all happen. Such questions seem far too banal for something so transcendent.

Still, how is all this going to work?

Given that we don't have Jesus physically with us, how are we going to learn his trade?

If this is an apprenticeship, who is the teacher?

In the same way that the Story of the Call causes us to imagine that our station might be the workshop of our apprenticeship, so the same Story calls us to be open to the Spirit using the form and the voice of others around us to assist us in our vocation as a disciple. As Athene spoke to Telemachus through Mentor, Jesus speaks to us through our mentors.

From the first moment of the Story of the Call, it is clear that an inescapable part of being a disciple is also being a disciple-maker. The fishermen are called to follow Jesus *and* catch others for the kingdom. The leper cannot help but tell everyone he meets about Jesus. The tax collector immediately throws a party with all his other 'sinner' friends so that they can be called too.

Even if you trace this theme back to the first call God makes in the Bible, it is there. When God first speaks to Abram, God gives the twofold promise: 'Come, follow me out of your country. I will bless you *so that* you will be a blessing!'[9]

---

9 Genesis 12:1–3.

From that moment, God's primary way of intervening in the world is through the people who have accepted his call. The invisible God is seen in people who do his will and is heard in people who speak his words.

To prove my point, I will make you a wager: I bet that you have had three mentors. That's right, without knowing you, I would hazard a guess that you have had at least three other people that have been for you what Mentor was for Telemachus. Stop and name them, those great souls who have spoken 'winged words' of peace, comfort, challenge and wisdom. Those people who God has embodied to speak to you.

If we follow this through to its obvious conclusion, we arrive at a humbling thought. To take this seriously means that not only must we be open to God appearing and speaking to us through others, but we must also be open to the Spirit using *our* form and *our* voice to guide others as they respond to their vocation as a disciple. You, too, may be a mentor to another. Indeed, it is part of the apprenticeship. One cannot learn to be like Jesus without learning how to bring the presence of the divine into contact with people in their everyday life.

So consider then, what if you understood that as part of your apprenticeship, your vocation would be to do this for three other people across your life? That's it. That is the job of your lifetime. Not to run a denomination or a church or even a small group. Just three people. In the average life span, that is not even one a decade.

But what if we all took this seriously? Actually, what if not all of us took this seriously? What if only forty of us took this seriously?

The missiologist Alan Hirsch calculates what would happen if forty people took up the calling to grow three people as apprentices of Jesus, and then if each of those three 'paid it forward' in discipling three more. He discovered that if this cycle kept repeating, it would only take about twenty-five cycles to disciple a population the size of America.

If the movement continued to grow, the population of the world would experience the blessing of a mentor in about thirty-seven years.[10]

3

40

7,000,000,000

37 years

In this way, the Story of the Call is not just about Jesus' call for us to become his follower-apprentices. It is also about us calling out – like the vexed Telemachus or the desperate leper – and the Divine touching our lives through human form. Furthermore, it is about the cry of our brothers and sisters in the human race and the possibility that, like Mentor or like Jesus himself, our form and our voice may become the embodiment of the Divine for a person (or three) who needs it.

---

10 Alan Hirsch, *The Forgotten Ways* (Grand Rapids: Brazos Press, 2006). You can watch Hirsch speak about this at http://www.youtube.com/watch?v=HELlLaXj3kk.

Finding our way: The first and second questions

The beauty of stories is that they leave us with questions. With each new story we will consider the key questions that we are left to ask about our apprenticeship. These questions are essentially timeless. You can return to them year after year, or even day after day, and potentially address them in new ways.

The Story of the Call presents us with our first two questions:

Where am I?

The Story of the Call depicts Jesus calling people in the context of their everyday lives. Likewise, we are invited to become disciples of Jesus right where we are, rather than in some ideal place where we are meant to be. This first question causes us to reflect upon the current settings, roles, activities and relationships of our lives, and imagine how they might become the workshop in which we learn our apprenticeship.

Who might be my three?

The Call to learn to become more like Jesus simultaneously activates two further calls. The first is the call that we make for people to help show us the Way. The second is the call that the needs of others makes towards us. In both cases, Jesus chooses to answer these calls through his apprentices, who embody Jesus to others. This question inspires us to reflect on who in our life is showing us the way of Jesus as well as to whom we might be sent to do the same.

The Story of the Relationship

Mark 2:18–4:34

Featuring ...

Backdrop: unshrunk junk

XII

Thicker than blood

Organismic

The way today: more time with less people

The way today: sacks of salt

Finding our way: the third and fourth questions

Backdrop: unshrunk junk

Mark 2:18–22

In words as fashion the same rule will hold;
Alike fantastic, if too new or old:
Be not the first by which the new are tried,
Nor the last to lay the old aside.
—Alexander Pope

I have only been on trend once in my life. It was in my first few years of primary school. Needless to say, I peaked early.

The trend at the time was marbles. I can't even remember why or how but I had lots of marbles. In fact, I had more marbles than any other person at my school. Every day I would transport a drawstring sack the size of a melon and the weight of a toolbox all the way to and from school. At lunchtime, I became a central figure in the school. I would trade with other children, growing my collection. I also gained the status of expert and judge and had peers come to me to arbitrate their trades. I was the Godfather of the marble trend for those few months.

But, alas, this is the best I can claim. Since that day I have missed virtually every trend that has come and gone. I never collected Pokémon. I never tried the Atkins diet when it was in, and I'm still not entirely sure what Paleo means. I never planked or even got invited to do the ice bucket challenge. I don't think I've ever written something on a Facebook page. No matter how hard I've tried, I do not find vampires erotic, like certain novels and movies seemed to assume that I would. And you'll probably just have to take my word for it that if I ever dress according to a trend, I am only ever doing it a few years after that trend passed.

The community of Jesus' apprentices is not immune to trends either. In my few decades of being involved in Christianity, I have seen numerous trends come and go in the world of discipleship. I have been involved in small groups, study groups, cell groups and home groups. I have been involved in churches that define themselves as anything from seeker sensitive to purpose driven to emerging. I sat through meetings where we've argued whether we should be mega or whether we should be messy. I have witnessed people trying the Jabez prayer, the Daniel diet and the fleece of Gideon. I've watched as we've journaled, and we've fasted, and every second year we have flocked to the new trendsetter when he or she has come to town.

And perhaps the greatest sin you can commit is to not be on trend! Those who resist the fads regularly feel like they are part of the 'out' group at high school. If you are not wearing or doing the right thing, everyone is glaring at you with exasperated sighs asking, 'Why not?'

This section of the Story of Discipleship starts with Jesus facing such a culture of trends. It sets the backdrop for the whole section. The trend here is fasting. The question was the same one that every trend follower asks every person who lags behind: 'Jesus, about fasting. We're doing it, they're doing it. The only people who aren't doing it are *your* disciples. *Why (the hell) not?'*

Jesus replies with full intellectual force. His answers are the rabbinic equivalent of three, quickfire, knockout strikes.

Firstly, this isn't the right time. Gloom and doom are not for the bride and groom. You are so busy with your spiritual trend that you are missing what God is doing right now: arriving to consummate the marriage between him and his people.[1]

Secondly, new and old don't mix. Patches unshrunk don't sew well on junk. We know that the old has some rips in it. Try to patch it up with this trend and it will only make things worse. Use new fabric to make a brand-new garment.

Finally, new things need new skins. Jesus' Way won't just fit into the 'way we've always done things'. This is a new norm, so it will need a new form. A new skin.

---

[1] The image of God coming into a marriage-like relationship with his people is a theme throughout the Old Testament. Just some examples are Jeremiah 31:31–33, Ezekiel 16:8–14 and Isaiah 54:5.

We don't need another fad, another craze, another trend. We have had enough secret recipes and step-by-step strategies.

In this part of the story, Jesus renews it all, from understandings of religious practices and theology (which, sadly, I do not have space for in this book), all the way through to our understanding of discipleship (which, thankfully, will be our focus). If we come along with him, we will learn that his way is far more demanding, less efficient and more painful than any trend.

Yet, it was the Way of our Rabbi. And, as we will see, it will cause us to imagine what might happen if we slow down, quieten down and pass the salt to those we find at the table. But these are all spoilers – first we must read the story.

XII

Mark 3:13–19

When you were at school, was there a place where the naughty kids would go to do naughty things? Was it behind the sports shed? Or was it around the bike racks? Maybe on the other side of the oval? I'm sure there was a place. And that place became a code word for the type of activity that the person was doing. For example, if someone said to meet them behind the sports shed, you probably knew that it wasn't to study for next week's exam.

In the story before us, Jesus goes to such a place: the mountains. The hills and mountains of Galilee were infamous for being a place where revolution started.[2] Revolutionaries would gather there to plot and plan, and they would retreat there for refuge and respite. Thus, when Jesus makes his way into the hills of Galilee to pray, people are expecting a movement – maybe even a revolution – to result.

So how does Jesus spend his time in the mountains? He uses it to call and appoint 12 people.

Twelve.

12.

XII.

However you want to write it, the number is important. Other New Testament writers also record this event, but they differ on various issues.[3] They disagree on when and in what context Jesus appointed this special group. They even disagree on who exactly was in this group.

What they don't disagree on is the number. Always 12. Why was this detail so important, even more important than the actual names of who was in that group?

Just like places can mean something, numbers can as well.

---

2 Tom Wright, *Mark for Everyone* (London: SPCK, 2004), 34.

3 For example, Matthew 10:1–4 or Luke 6:12–16.

1   13   A million   3.14   9/11

I imagine that many of those numbers, if not all, represent something to you. Of course, there would also be other numbers uniquely significant for you. Take, for instance, your date of birth, wedding anniversary, telephone number or credit card digits.

So, when Jesus gathered and appointed 12, there was an unmistakable meaning involved: he was rebooting the family of Jacob, also known as Israel. The nation of Israel was a family of 12 tribes descended from Jacob's 12 sons. Now, it was beginning again, right from the ground level.

Think back to the story of Abraham, Isaac and Jacob. When God stepped into human history to set it right, what did he do? He did not build a city or an empire. He did not appoint a king or elect a government. He did not call a teacher or a guru or a prophet. Instead, God chose a family.

Not even a famous family. Not even a powerful family. Not even a fertile family. A family that was chosen and appointed: blessed to be a blessing to the whole world. This was and is the point of God choosing Israel. It was not God playing favourites; it was God on a mission.

When Jesus came to fulfil that mission, he also rejected the way of government, empire and industry, even though all those options were available to him. His revolution was different. His revolution was about turning back to the original plan. To start a family through whom every nation would be blessed. It was *this* that was the true revolution that started in the mountains of Galilee.

As Phillip Yancey insightfully comments, the focus of our society 'has shifted from families to institutions. Yet the New Testament stubbornly presents the church as being more like a family than an institution'.[4] This forces us to reflect: when we think of discipleship, does it look like what happens in a family or what happens in an institution?

---

4 Phillip Yancey, *Church: Why Bother?* (Grand Rapids: Zondervan, 2001), 62.

Thicker than blood

Mark 3:31–34

There is the famous phrase: 'blood is thicker than water'. It is generally used to mean that the relationships within families (i.e. blood relations) are a stronger and more important bond than the relationships outside of family (i.e. water relations). Of course, compared to the explanation, the proverb is so much more memorable for the image of dense, viscous blood sticking more than thin, runny water.

There are some cultures and stories that virtually treat this proverb as sacred. The genre-defining film *The Godfather* would be an obvious example. Everything that happens is for the sake of the family. From *Pride and Prejudice* to *Game of Thrones*, many stories depict the way families manoeuvre, act and sacrifice to maintain their honour and relationships.

If there ever was a culture that embodied this proverb *par excellence*, it would have to be the children of Israel. In the Ten Commandments, the first command that is not about worshipping God properly is about honouring your father and mother. This command was certainly saying more than 'be nice to your mum and dad'. From the time of that commandment, all the way through to when Jesus himself was teaching, the imperative to maintain the honour of your household and its elders was the underpinning principle of all personal and social interactions. It decided where you lived and what job you would do (imagine if you did not have a choice over even these matters?). It dictated who you were friends with and who you married (would you let your parents decide this for you?). It prescribed how you received guests and who you invited to parties, and it shaped the way you would do business and how you handled conflict. It was so powerful that the

Jewish communities throughout the Roman Empire were renowned for their sense of family.[5]

Blood is thicker than water.

So, as Jesus goes around the countryside doing all sorts of wonders, it is little surprise that Jesus' mother and brothers come looking for him. It was the only honourable thing to do. After all, there were even some rumours that Jesus of Nazareth was doing all of this by an evil spirit.

They needed to at least go to him. Perhaps talk some sense into him. Perhaps bring him home to where he belongs. After all, blood is thicker than water.

When Jesus' family arrive, they are forced to wait outside the crowded house. We have already seen one group hack through the roof to get their friend in front of Jesus' healing hands. Jesus' family would not have to do anything quite so dishonourable. They could simply send word inside and Jesus would let them in. Everyone in the crowd knew the deal. Middle Eastern hospitality is the same now as it was then.[6] The crowd would move aside and clear the places of most honour for the family of the rabbi. Food and drink would be brought immediately, as well as things for them to wash themselves with after the journey. No one would be offended, because blood is thicker than water.

I have never been in a situation where someone has said something as embarrassing, challenging or gut-twistingly, jaw-droppingly shocking as what Jesus says next:

'Who are my mother and my brothers?'

If there were people there who were wondering whether Jesus was mad or possessed, this might have clinched it for them.

Jesus points to the crowd and offers these words: 'Here they are! Here is my family! My brother, my sister and my mother is anyone who does God's will'.

---

5 Alfred Edersheim, *Sketches of Jewish Social life in the days of Christ* (Grand Rapids: Eerdmans, 1985), 123.

6 Kenneth Bailey, *Jesus through Middle Eastern Eyes* (Downers Grove: IVP Academic, 2008).

Doesn't he know the proverb?

Perhaps he did. You see, the phrase we have, and its assumed meaning, is actually a distortion of the proverb in its original form. It morphed slowly, perhaps even deliberately, like a centuries-long version of the children's game Telephone. In its original form, the proverb read: 'The blood of the covenant is thicker than the water of the womb'.

In other words, the bonds you make through a covenant – a blood binding agreement – are actually thicker than those that exist by the mere random draw of birth.

The new family of God – chosen to bless all nations – would be defined along such lines. When Jesus finished his life and ministry, the community that he left in his wake was one that transcended all religious, ethnic, economic and gender lines. The blood of this new covenant was thicker than the water of the womb.

Organismic

Mark 4:1–34

Time is money, so we are told. But do we really believe it? Well, the English language suggests that we do.

We *make* time, and we *spend* time. We also *buy* time when we need it. We can live on *borrowed* time. An inconvenience can *cost* you time. We also talk endlessly about how we can *save* time, lest we become time *poor*. If you are savvy, you will also know how to *invest* your time, *budget* your time and even use your time *profitably*.[7]

This is just one example of the way a central metaphor in our culture will shape our language. This then shapes our thoughts, which in turn shapes our choices. What if we thought of time as music? We would speak of listening to time, reading time, keeping in rhythm with time, creating harmony with time, keeping in tune with time, and even playing time. How would that change the choices we make?

In our Christian communities at this current time in history, we have a similarly powerful central metaphor: salvation is a transaction.

How is this reflected in our language? Consider the following statement of the gospel:

> Our sin has put us into *debt* with God. The *price* that we have to *pay* for our rebellion is death and hell. However, God loved the world so much that he *offered* his own son to *pay* for our sins. This *cost* Jesus his life. Therefore, we have the *free* gift of salvation, which we can *receive* through repentance and faith.

Does this sound familiar? There may be some slight differences, but on the whole, I would say that you have heard a similar speech before. You may be thinking, 'So what? That's the gospel, isn't it?'

---

7 George Lakoff & Mark Johnson, *Metaphors We Live By* (Chicago: University of Chicago Press, 1980).

Well, maybe it's a version of the gospel. Certainly, it is not unbiblical. At times, the New Testament compares salvation to a type of transaction, for example, the buying back of a slave (ransom) or paying the price for something valuable.[8] However, every metaphor has a 'yes' or 'no' factor. To say that God is like a rock is to affirm God's dependability, strength and assuredness; it is not to say God is unfeeling, or immovable, or harsh. In this instance, the transaction metaphors of the New Testament communicate our worth to God and the price he is willing to pay for us.

There is a danger to how central this message has become. For example, the first time I presented this thought was to a group of pastors at a minister's conference. When I read out the exact same example of the 'transactional gospel' that I wrote above, one of the pastors asked me to remind him of which passage of Scripture written by Paul that I was quoting. You see, even to this *pastor*, those few sentences were so taken for granted that he thought they were a direct quote from the Bible!

So that's the danger! We presume that salvation is a transaction just like we presume that time is money. This is because the world we live in is dominated by economics. It is a world of buying and selling; making and trading; loans and debts; and saving and spending. We can seriously make anything: time, sense, peace, love, babies, or any number of other things. In the same way, it has come to pass that our faith talk follows a similar line.

This was not always so. When Rabbi Jesus sits down to finally say, 'This is what the kingship of God is like ...', he does not use the language of transaction. Instead he uses the language of the organic ...

It is like scattered seed, on all different types of ground, which then dies or thrives.

It is like a dark room transformed into light as a lamp is placed on a stand.

---

8 For example, Matthew 20:28 and 13:44–46.

It is a seed mysteriously, secretly rising day and night until it is a plant ready for harvest.

It is the smallest of seeds growing to the biggest shrub in the garden, serving the birds.

There is not a dollar or cent in sight. For Jesus, there was a different concept at work. For him, salvation is not a transaction.

Salvation is a transformation.

It is better explained in the language of change and growth; revolution and restoration; of organisms and life. It means that salvation was not just a moment that happened in the past or a moment to look forward to in the future. It is a process that is happening daily. If salvation is a transaction, discipleship is an afterthought. If salvation is a transformation, discipleship is the first, second and final thought, just as it was for Jesus.

So, what would it be like for us to change our language? How would that in turn shape our thoughts? And then our choices?

What would it be like if our churches were not just containers, holding people until they reached the end of their lives? What if our churches were greenhouses, places to grow and thrive? What if they were Petri dishes in which new life forms were evolving?

What if they were the fertile soil in which disciples grew?

For those of us who have tried transactional Christianity and have been left with familiar buyer's remorse, it is time for us to consider a way of being that is organic and organismic. But be aware: if we want new wine, then we will also need new wineskins.

The way today: more time with less people

At the heart of the Story of the Relationship lies some of the core values of the Way of Jesus:

Jesus prizes the relational over the institutional, transformations over transactions, and organisms over organisations.

So how do we live that story? How do we write the Story of the Relationship in our time and place?

Firstly, we have to return to where we started: unshrunk cloth and new wineskins. If we are going to live this story – prizing relationships, blood covenants and organic growth at a higher value than institutions, formal settings and organisations – then we cannot just sew this new piece of cloth onto our old garment. We cannot put this new wine into our old wineskin. We need to change our form in order to change our norm.

In my experience, when a church launches a discipleship initiative, it is usually one or a combination of the following three categories:

Information-based discipleship initiatives most often come in the form of a course, a book, a sermon series or a system (e.g. something that sounds like, 'The Five Keys to Prayer'). The implicit value in these approaches is that change and/or growth comes through data delivered principally to our rational brains. They are often taught from an 'expert' to a group of people less educated than themselves, that is, the 'jug to mug' approach.

Time limited discipleship initiatives usually run for a set amount of time. The time limit varies, but it rarely goes beyond the length of a year. Most are shorter. Emphasis is on completion or graduation. The implicit value is on the immediacy of change.

Mass delivered discipleship initiatives are usually designed to reach a large number at once, often an entire church community. Again, this will then usually need to take on the form of the expert lecturer speaking to an anonymous mass. The value here is on efficiency, or in other words, getting the most 'bang for your buck'.

These three categories are our old wineskins. Of course, I cannot guarantee that your church community has experienced this, but I would bet that most people reading this will resonate with this at least on some level. I bet that the last time your church tried to 'do discipleship' it was information-based, time limited and mass delivered.

So, what would it look like if we sought to do discipleship in the most relational, slow and inefficient way possible? What if every minister in the country considered how she or he could be less efficient?

The very thought probably grinds against you, like a cog in a machine trying to turn a different way. But if your goal is transformation rather than transaction, then things are not always efficient.

A friend of mine once commented that 'human growth is glacial'. Think of the way a new human life comes into the world. Human beings are comparatively inefficient breeders. Basically, we can have one child a year. Compared to rats, rabbits, dogs, cats, ants, cockroaches and probably a whole legion of other species, we do not reproduce quickly. Furthermore, an infant is born in absolute need of its caregivers. Our path to independence is long and slow. And yet that inefficiency enables a whole range of higher functions. The slowness forces us to connect and attach to each other in a way that a cockroach could not even conceptualise. It forces us to teach at the pace that we learn.[9]

What if we tried to speed it up? What if we expected a newborn to talk, walk or use a fork, and we put them in situations that required these skills? And yet we wonder why there is such a lack of growth of apprentice-followers in our churches! We expect a six-week course to do the trick. We expect that our forty-day commitment will be enough. We expect that this sermon series is what will finally change people.

---

[9] If you want to see this in a stunning presentation, look up the name Deb Roy and his TED Talk 'The Birth of a Word': https://www.ted.com/talks/deb_roy_the_birth_of_a_word?language=en.

Dawson Trotman, the founder of the Navigators ministry (one of the most relational focused ministries of the last century), once put the point perfectly. He said, 'If Jesus' way teaches us anything, it is this: more time with less people makes a greater impact for God's kingdom'.

More time with less people. That is the new wineskin. Remember that the challenge was for you to be a mentor to three people in your lifetime. That doesn't even equate to one a year. It doesn't even equate to one per decade! You've got time. Use it!

What might this new wineskin look like in practice? Let me give an example, not as a definitive model, but rather just to stimulate your imagination. For the past few years I have been involved in planting a new church community in one of the fastest developing suburbs of Brisbane. In the early days there was just a few of us; we were small enough to fit around a dining room table. When we began to meet together, we realised that we had a unique opportunity to set things up in a new way. In other words, we were not just going to try to squeeze this new wine into an old wineskin.

So we made a few changes to the usual community gatherings of a church. For instance, we meet on a Friday night rather than a Sunday morning, because that was what the people said was working for them.

We also did something that I have never regretted. Usually, a church service is mainly ritual followed by a smaller amount of relationship time. We (generously) estimated the standard ratio to be about seventy-five per cent ceremony to twenty-five per cent relationship time. So, in the spirit of the relational ministry of Jesus (how much of the gospel depicts Jesus leading a worship service?), we reversed that ratio. For the two hours that we meet on a Friday night, we spend an hour and a half (seventy-five per cent) of it in activities that promote relationships (e.g. children's games, BBQs, cups of coffee and chats), and only half an hour (twenty-five per cent) in ceremony.

An overwhelming majority of the people who come to that community are not from a Christian background and have not been connected with a faith community before. But we are determined that the seeds we are sowing will fall into good soil – not shallow or stony ground that will thwart real growth. Therefore, we take the long, slow process of tilling the earth. We are determined to form deep roots so that there can be great fruit; fruit that will last.

That community is still new. It has been born, and is certainly crawling, and I imagine over the coming years it will be taking its first few wobbly steps. But what is clear is that deep in its DNA is a priority on growing at the pace of life – the slow, inefficient pace of relationships.

More time with less people.

The way today: a sack of salt

When I was nineteen years old, I had been the youth worker at my church for just over a year and a half. For a while before that, there had been little deliberate youth ministry in that community, so the ministry was fairly green. Not to mention that I was green. As green as an apple. I was making things up as I went along (and I still am).

My church sponsored me to go to a youth ministry conference and, while there, I sat in on a workshop by one of the most experienced and committed disciplers of young people in the country, Tim Hawkins. At the end of the workshop, I casually approached Tim and presented him with the situation of my ministry at the time: a community of about ten to twenty young people, many of whom were very committed, with a close connection to a school of over two thousand students and a connection to a fairly conservative but supportive congregation.

Tim's advice, which naturally he would not remember, was seriously priceless: 'Spend some time praying and discerning which two or three of your young people might become leaders in the future and spend eighty per cent of your time with them. Everything else you do is secondary to this.' Priceless. I wish I could pay him back for this advice but I would never have the money to match the value of this wisdom.

As it turned out, I was only in that ministry for a little more than a year after this happened. But in that year, I followed his advice. I poured myself into those relationships. And, as Dawson Trotman would put it, as I spent more time with less people, I saw how it truly made a greater impact for God's kingdom.

Consider this. Those two or three young people became youth leaders themselves, continuing the youth ministry after I left. They were all leaders within their school and impacted their peers through the honesty and sincerity of their faith, their committed service and, in particular, using their creative talents to share the message of their faith. In their adult life they have been equally as active in the life of their church communities as they have been in mission to those not-yet Christians. One was even the president of the largest Christian group at the largest university in his state.

As it turned out, many years later my wife and I had the opportunity of connecting with them again and, for a second time, nurturing them as apprentice-followers of Jesus for over two years during weekly meetings in our home. Now, they have all moved again, starting their professions and spreading the pollen of the gospel to new cities and new states. One is about to embark on a ministry of planting churches. Another is a full-time youth worker. Another still, an international missionary.

Now, I would not be so arrogant as to think these events happened because of the time I spent with these young people. I was more like a spectator on the sidelines applauding their feats. But if I had any influence, this was the form it took: many hours, over many years, with many meals (pizza in the early days, cups of tea more recently), many conversations, much listening, some talking and no regrets.

Aristotle once wrote that the only certain way to make friends with someone is to eat a sack of salt together.

By saying this, of course he did not mean that two people should sit down with a sack of salt and eat until the bag is empty. Instead, he was thinking of the tiny pinch of salt you add to a meal. Thus, to be friends with someone, you need to have shared enough meals with that person to use up a whole sack of salt, pinch by pinch.

You don't eat a sack of salt in a forty-day course or a six-week sermon series. If you are serious about following the call of Jesus to help others grow as apprentice-followers, then you need to be prepared to eat a sack of salt with someone.

Perhaps you still doubt me. Perhaps you still think that discipleship can be done in short-term, information rich, relationally poor modalities. Maybe it can.

Then my only question for you is that if this is true, then why did Jesus, the anointed Son of God, spend three years with just a handful of people? Why did he choose family as his model, with all of the implications of lifelong relationships? Why, when asked, did he liken the kingdom of God to a seed growing slowly, waiting patiently until the right season? Do we really think we can do it better than Jesus? Faster than Jesus? With more people than Jesus?

I cannot read the gospels and think otherwise: the way of more time with less people, and the way of a sack of salt, is the Way of the Rabbi.

Finding our way: The third and fourth questions

In seeking to live out the Story of the Relationship in our lives, we are called to consider two further questions of discipleship:

Who are the few?

The Way of Jesus prioritises spending more time with less people. As apprentices of this Way, we do well to reflect upon who in our life might resemble the types of relationships Jesus categorises as his 'new family': those relationships marked by the slow pace of life. This question offers us the opportunity to reflect upon those who might be the 'few' with whom we will be spending the most time as part of our apprenticeship.

When's dinner?

Given our need to eat a sack of salt, this question asks us to consider when in our life we will have the quality time to spend with these few people. It may not be a meal, but we need to identify where our lives might regularly cross over in a way that gives us the time to give real input into each other's apprenticeship. This time might occur naturally or it might have to be organised. Either way, we should see each and every little interaction as a meal that sustains us on the journey of following Jesus. Pinch by pinch, we use up the sack of salt.

The Story of the Adventure

Mark 4:35–8:30

Featuring ...

Backdrop: who has the greater faith?

Show-and-go

Sharing a miracle

Hospital passes

The way today: do something!

The way today: action first, words later

Finding our way: the fifth and sixth questions

Backdrop: who has the greater faith?

Mark 4:35–41

It can be amazing to see someone share a carefully honed skill or hard-earned piece of expertise. I love to hear a piano tuner talk about pianos, or a gardener talk about plants, or even someone share their research, no matter what the field. I know how excited I get when someone asks me to share an area of personal expertise. A sudden excitement wriggles inside me; I feel eager to share what I know and what I can do. This is especially the case among friends and family. It is an honour to use our expertise to serve those we love most dearly. Above anything else, it helps us feel that we matter.

Jesus certainly knew what his disciples could do. As we saw in the Story of the Call, he knew they were fishermen. He knew that their skills as fishermen were going to be used under the kingship of God where they would be catching people into the good news. He also knew their skills as men of the sea. He had them prepared to row him to safety in case the pressing crowd became dangerous.[1] He also taught from a boat, with the crowd on the shore.[2] As Kenneth Bailey rightly points out, a boat in water does not make a very stable pulpit and most likely the disciples would have been at the oars, exercising minute movements to keep the boat as still as possible for the rabbi to teach.[3] Surely those disciples felt their chests swell at the chance to exhibit their long-practised seamanship while serving the cause of God's kingdom. For all those years they spent wondering if they even mattered, they now had an answer.

Then, one day in the middle of their apprenticeship, Jesus came to them for their skills and announces: 'Let us go over to the other side'. These words meant physically crossing the lake but they also

---

[1] Mark 3:9.

[2] Mark 4:1.

[3] Bailey, *Jesus Through Middle Eastern Eyes*.

symbolically meant crossing the world. They would be travelling out of Jewish territory and into the unknown. They were taking the kingdom into new territory. Foreign territory. Hostile territory. This was going to be an adventure.

Were they still painted with pride? Or was the facade starting to crack under the heat of fearful questions? What would they find on the other side? And what about coming back? Would they be accepted, having been to such places? Their rabbi was already having his sanity questioned. What would this do?

Yet, take note that Jesus shows no such fear. Instead, he steps into the boat, curls up in the bow and leaves the sailing to the sailors. Even when the thunder starts, he sleeps in absolute ease with his disciples at the helm. The wind tears at the sails and wave after wave slaps against the feeble wood of the boat. Jesus sleeps on, as content as an infant slumbering in her car seat as her mother drives a dangerous road. Trust. Complete trust.

The disciples, however, are not so sure. They may not have been sure of the journey to begin with. Maybe this is a sign, even a sign from God. Didn't God send a storm when Jonah went the wrong way? Jesus' faith is perceived as disinterest. Callousness. Like a commander dining after giving the battle orders. 'Don't you care?' was their scream to wake him and to accuse him.

So, Jesus wakes. He rises, and he roars his rebuke over the noise. He rebukes the storm first. It smarts at the words, whimpering into retreat. But then he rebukes his apprentices. 'Have you no faith?' is his accusation in reply. The disciples are left with a new question on their lips: who is this man? (Remember the secret call of the prologue? By the end of the Story of the Adventure, they will have their answer for this question.)

Jesus has called his apprentices. He has made them family through covenant. Now he is about to take them into new territory. This is the Story of the Adventure. And it cannot be understood unless you understand one eternal equation. It is like the story is encrypted unless we have this code to unlock it…

Jesus has more faith in his disciples than his disciples have in him.

Time after time he is surprised by their lack of understanding and their slowness to trust him. Time after time they are surprised that Jesus can actually do what he can do. In other words, Jesus expects more from them than they expect from him.

This should not surprise us, but it does. In our modern discourse, when we use the word 'faith' we are most often talking about human trust in God. But in the Bible, especially the Old Testament, the faithful one is God. God's faithfulness goes far beyond any human faith. God has more faith in us than we have in God. God trusts us more than we trust God. God believes in us more than we believe in God. In fact, the basic problems of the world stem from the mismatch of God's faith and our faith.

When God creates the earth, he puts the stewardship of it into human hands. Every time God acts to save, he does so through human agents, from Noah to Abraham and Sarah to Joseph to Moses to Ruth to the judges and the prophets, all the way through to Mary and Joseph. In every instance God is, in some way, let down. It always seems to be that while God places the fate of his creation in human hands, human beings struggle to place their own will into God's hands. Yet God remains faithful, both to his promises and to his plan. Hence, when Israel turns to worship in the songs of the psalms, they plead to God and praise his faithfulness.

Is it any wonder then that Jesus in his ministry follows this same pattern? The story of Jesus and his apprentices is the story of Israel before and the church after. It is our story. It is our adventure. The faithful God and the fearful followers forever called to journey together into new territory.

Show-and-go

Mark 5:1–6:13

I'm hopeless with directions, especially when someone just tells me where to go. I just sit there nodding, knowing that not a single sentence is sticking long enough in my brain to be of any real use. I defy the male stereotype. I would happily use maps, do U-turns and ask for help. Best of all is if someone can show me the way, then I can do it by myself the next time I need to go.

Therefore, I have always marvelled at the lives of explorers. For instance, take the Austrian skydiver Felix Baumgartner. In 2012, I was utterly captivated by the project to take Baumgartner to the edge of space and then parachute – yes, *parachute* – back to Earth. Along with thousands of others worldwide, I watched the live stream of Baumgartner standing at the edge of his pod, high enough to see the curved horizon of the Earth's sphere, high enough to make the land below nothing more than an indistinguishable canvas of block colours, and high enough to make all sorts of questions surge through your mind. He was at the edge of uncharted territory. No one had jumped from this height. No one had ever been in freefall for as long as he was going to be. No one had ever used their unprotected body to break the sound barrier as he was going to do.

So, along with the thousands around the world, I sat and watched as Felix Baumgartner stood at the edge of knowledge, and then took one step further.[4]

Even to this day, my stomach involuntarily rises with weightlessness to see Baumgartner silently fall from his pod.

Yet that is what explorers do. By definition, they only exist in a state of being lost. They deliberately move themselves to the utter edge of what anyone knows, and then they take one step further.

---

4 The video footage is all over the internet, and a simple search of the name 'Felix Baumgartner' will lead you to a recording of this very moment.

It is such a moment that we see in Mark's Story of the Adventure. The storm behind them, Jesus and his apprentices land their boat in the country of the Gerasenes. It is an unclean land. A land where they even herd pigs.

Then, in the spirit of all explorers, they stand at the edge of the shore and take one step further onto land, bodies tense and eyes wide for what will happen next.

In the distance they see a man running towards them. He tears towards the shore at a manic speed. He carries evil in his spirit. He comes from the cave tombs. He is the demon of the town – the man you tell your kids about. He can tear chains apart, link from link. He howls at night and cuts himself until bloody.

And he knows Jesus. They meet, face to face, and Jesus banishes this spirit from him.

The town is amazed, yet also fearful, so Jesus is forced to return back across the lake. Even so, the adventure continues. A woman is healed just from the touch of his clothes. He even wakes a girl from death as easily as he would wake her from sleep.

Then Jesus' journey goes to a place that many, many people avoid returning to: home. There he is met not just with doubt, but also suspicion. People do not trust him. They know the soil he grew out of, and they cannot bring themselves to eat the fruit he is producing. So, he leaves without being able to do the things that he has done elsewhere, even on the 'other side'. We need to look long and hard into Jesus' human eyes to see the word that is recorded to describe his reaction: amazed.

As the rabbi bravely takes God's reign into new territory, Mark takes great pains to make us aware of what would seem like an insignificant detail: that the disciples are with him every step of the way. Jesus casts out demons … and his disciples are there. Jesus heals the sick … and his disciples are with him. He raises the dead. He is rejected by those who know him. And his disciples are there with him. Even when the crowds are dismissed, they are there. Even when Jesus goes off 'alone', they are there. When he needs a break, they are there, still bathing in the dust of his feet.

Little do they know that their job is not just to witness the adventure. It is not until the rabbi gathers the 12, splits them into six groups of pairs and sends them out like explorers that they realise the meaning of all of this. Suddenly, there they are, with not a cent in their pockets, with their fate in the hands of the families they visit and nothing but a word of authority. They are at the edge of all they know to be safe. And then they take one step further ...

What is Jesus asking them to do? Nothing more than what he has already done in their presence. They are called to announce that God has come to reign on earth as in heaven, to heal the sick, to speak the truth to evil powers and to face either acceptance or rejection in the towns they encounter.

Just take a moment to consider the people he is sending. They are as ordinary as they come. Ordinary, some even dishonourable, professions. No resources. No qualifications. Even more remarkably for our modern minds is that by our usual criteria for conversion (the Engel Scale, for example), they are not yet even Christian. Yet Jesus is prepared to send them. They have all the training they need in what they have witnessed.

They have seen the show. Now it is their turn to go.

When we come to grow others as apprentice-followers of Jesus, how do we normally do it? Do we use a show-and-go approach as Jesus did? Or do we just use a learn-and-repeat method? If they can give us the right answers, are they then disciples? And if they can't, what do we do? Talk louder? Talk more? Give up?

Remember that discipleship is an apprenticeship, not a degree. Lectures, readings and written exams will not do. At some stage, the master will have to hand over her tools to the apprentice and let the apprentice try out the things she or he has seen.

Just this week, I had to confront my discomfort and try this. One of the communities of disciples that I am called to lead meets in a home once a week during the evening. One of the members of this community approached me asking to lead the study. I was reluctant. Reluctant about this person's ability, reluctant to take the risk, reluctant to give up my control. But he had been watching me and others doing this for some years now. When he came to do this, he was well prepared, humble, facilitative and sensitive. In fact, he made me reflect upon my own practice of teaching.

So, I wonder how many apprentices of Jesus have been merely watching or listening to discipleship their whole life. I wonder what would happen if we stopped giving directions and allowed people to take a step out into what they are yet to know ...

Sharing a miracle

Mark 6:30–44

Compassion may well be the most misunderstood thing in human existence.

Don't get me wrong, I believe in compassion. In fact, I base much of my life on compassion. However, I do not understand why people praise it, crave it or idealise it. Compassion is far from being a shiny thing. It is messy at best and painful at its wrenching worst.

In truth, compassion goes against our instinct. Consider this: you are walking through the crowded city streets during the morning rush hour on your way to work. The crowd smells of black coffee, aftershave and perfume, and clean clothes. You are late already, so you start angling towards the side of the path, so you can find a quicker route around the edge. As you get to the periphery and start to accelerate your stride, you see someone sitting on the ground. It is a young man, his face lopsided with deformity, begging on the street.

Without breaking stride, your eyes respond by both natural instinct and social training, and they look away.

You look away. Not because you are unkind or uncaring. Quite the opposite. You look away because you are empathetic. Because you recognise the pain immediately. You look away because your neural circuits are able to recreate the pain of another within your own psychology and physiology, even without experiencing the pain yourself. And our body's most natural response to pain is to get rid of it as soon as possible. So, we look away.

Compassion goes against this instinct. Compassion calls us to look at the pain and not to blink. Compassion calls us to stop. To care. No matter what it costs us.

The story we are about to read is a story of compassion. Apart from the event of the resurrection, the only other miracle that is recorded in all four gospels is the feeding of the five thousand people. I'm not surprised. Firstly, there were naturally many witnesses, so there were plenty of people to pass the story on. Furthermore, this miracle would not have been forgotten by the disciples, given how close they were to the action. Any attempt to tell the story of this miracle as being by Jesus alone – with the disciples airbrushed out – is to render the story wrong.

In this way, this miracle represents the pattern of every disciple who sees a need but does not look away.

The story begins late in the day. The crowd have swarmed to Jesus, drawn by his compassion, travelling a long distance just to hear him. Jesus' compassion has led him to teach them, even late into the day. But … they are nowhere. Their place has no name. It is not a town and not a settlement. It is wilderness.

It is the disciples, not Jesus, who point out the elephant in the room. Night is falling, people are far from home and they are hungry. The disciples have spent enough time with Jesus to learn how to look at a crowd with compassionate eyes. They offer him a solution: send the people away so they can go and find their own food. There is an implicit avoidance in their request – 'Send the people, but don't send us!'

This represents the call of every disciple who does not look away. Helpless and even hopeless, we call to God to take both their pain and our pain away. But we are rarely prepared for how God responds.

Jesus acknowledges the problem but offers a different solution. 'You give them something to eat', he says. Remember that Jesus has more faith in his disciples that his disciples have in him. They do not ask for a miracle of him, but he asks for a miracle from them. This is what every disciple, from Moses onwards, hears when they bring the world's need to God: 'You have seen this for a reason, which is that you are part of the solution'. Still every disciple, from Moses until now, answers in the same way.

The disciples start to tell Jesus what they don't have. This time around it's the money but it could just as easily be the time. Or the qualifications. The interest. The energy. The freedom. The ability. The courage. The virtue. The strength. The knowledge. The support. The passion. The lifestyle. The opportunity. The know-how. The confidence.

Abraham: 'I'm too old'. David: 'I'm too young'. Esther: 'The king hasn't summoned me'. Isaiah: 'I have unclean lips'. Moses: 'I can't speak'. Joshua: 'I'm not Moses'. Whenever God calls us on his adventure, to be a miracle in this world, we always reply in a way like this. Not only does God have more faith in us than we have in God, but God has more faith in us than we have in ourselves.

Jesus ignores our doubts completely. The disciples could have talked for hours about what they didn't have (just as we still do today). Jesus knew what they didn't have when he invited them to feed the crowd. How boring, how utterly pointless, would it be to *talk* about that?

Jesus asks the one and only question we should be asking ourselves: What do you have? Or, even better, what have you been given? The disciples have to go and look for it. It isn't as obvious as what they don't have. But like all disciples who turn their attention from what they don't have to what they have been given, they make a discovery.

'We do have a little ...'

They come back with a small amount of food. Five lumps of carbs and two serves of protein. It is little, but it is something. They don't have nothing anymore. Once they see the little that they have, Jesus shows them what to do with it.

He accepts what is given. He gives thanks for it. He doesn't ask for more or question why there is so little. He is simply grateful. Then, he breaks it. One loaf becomes two. The two broken pieces become four as they are broken again. And break by break, division by division, the food is multiplied and shared among the crowd.

Finally, while it is Jesus who breaks the bread, it is the disciples who distribute it. They are the hands of the miracle. At the back of a crowd of over five thousand people, you would probably have missed the actions of Jesus; you would only see one of 12 come past with bread and fish for you and your family. They then go around again, gathering what is left over.

So this story is for all of you who see the needs of the world and who don't turn away. This is for those of you who choose compassion and feel the pain of your families, communities, church, country or even those you don't know.

This is for those of you who feel helpless and hopeless, and your list of things that you don't have goes on and on like an infinity loop.

For all of you who chose the messiness of compassion, this story is an invitation to look at the problems in your life, the church and the world, and to ask the only question that you ever need to ask ...

What have I been given?

If you want to stay exactly where you are, simply keep talking about what you don't have. But if you ask this question, be prepared to go on an adventure. If you take what you have been given, give thanks for it, share it and be prepared for things to multiply.

Even miraculously.

Hospital passes

Mark 7:1–8:30

In the parlance of sport, there is the curious saying of describing something as a 'hospital pass'. What turns a normal 'pass' into a 'hospital pass' is that the receiver takes possession of the ball just a split second before an opposition player arrives to make the tackle. In that moment, the receiver is utterly vulnerable: their code stipulates they must take the ball, however, with no time to pass, evade or protect themselves, they are left to take the full force of the opposition's aggression. Hence, the potential for a hospital to be involved.

There is a pay-off, however. To take a hospital pass and cop the full fury that it involves becomes something like a rite of passage. It is recognised that you have passed the test. You have upheld the qualities – even the virtues – that sport is meant to manifest: courage, team play, resilience. Something has changed about you, almost existentially.

There are moments in the Way of the Adventure that remind me of both sides of the experience of a hospital pass. They are moments of disequilibrium, disorientation and discomfort. Yet, they are equally moments of transition, transfiguration and transformation. If we have followed the call into this apprenticeship, we can expect hospital passes to come our way. No one can credibly follow Jesus presuming he only walks towards comfort and security.

The most transformative such experience for me occurred when I was just a young, long-haired, barely-shaven theology student walking through the pedestrian underpass of Central train station during the afternoon peak hour. At the edge of the crowd, I spotted the only man who was scruffier looking than me. He sat on the ground in his rags of clothes with two pieces of cardboard. He held the first in his hands, displaying his plea for charity; the other he placed on the ground to collect whatever people deigned to throw his way.

I would have been able to just walk past, except for the fact that in the previous week's lecture on building community we had been studying the way Jesus formed communities of justice. In that very lecture it had dawned on me that Jesus did not display the model of charity which we so often espouse. Put simply, Jesus did not feed the poor; rather, Jesus ate with the poor.

The thought was a hospital pass for me. There was nothing to do but to take it in both hands and cop whatever was coming as a result of it. So, with that thought in my head and with youthful idealism in my heart, I wiped the sweat off my palm, extended my hand and introduced myself to the man sitting on the floor of Central Station. Before I knew it, I was sitting with him on those cold and dirty tiles.

His name was Doug. He had a southern American accent, and the first thing he said to me was, 'You know, people are real _____!' (I've omitted the word, but if you think of the worst expletive you know, you're probably pretty close to the mark.) As a young Christian, with more than a streak of puritanism, I winced at the strength of the language. But he explained himself. 'You see all these people rushing past? Going from their city jobs to their suburban homes? Wearing nice suits? None of 'em givin' anything to me!'

These words got me watching the world from Doug's point of view. In time, empathy overcame discomfort. From our position on the floor, the crowd swelled around us like a stampeding herd. In response, we shrunk into the most diminutive space possible, pulling our limbs toward our bodies and bowing our heads for protection and anonymity. I now understood the posture of a beggar.

Glancing at the crowd, there were even some faces I recognised, but they didn't see me. The pain instinct meant that they looked away.

We talked for some time. We talked about his time as a soldier in Vietnam, about what I was studying, about places we had both been. What was at first strange was starting to become familiar …

… until, at one point, Doug turned to me and said, 'You know, you're a pretty good guy. If I ever get my hands on any weed, I'd be happy to share it with you'. At this comment, my inner purist returned with force. My head was swimming with all the social messages I'd been given about people who are homeless. I took his statement as a moral failure on his part, and my judgement was kindled.

Yet, while I floundered to give a response, a young woman, one of the well-dressed city yuppies, approached Doug and handed him a large muffin and a bottle of iced coffee. She smiled and simply said, 'I hope this helps'.

Well, it wasn't weed, but Doug was as good as his word. Though I never asked for it, he shared the gift with me. But to do this, he had to take hold of the muffin with his grimy, train station floor hands, insert his nicotine-stained fingers into the dough, and tear the muffin in half. A hundred ways of politely refusing the food came through my head but none of them seemed reasonable. Then, it was too late. The hospital pass had been passed. The defiled muffin was already in my hands and as I lifted it to my mouth, I wished I had never realised that Jesus ate with the poor.

Still, it wasn't over. The drink was still to come. He unscrewed the lid and lifted the plastic bottle to his cracked lips. I watched the iced coffee lap against his unshaven, unwashed whiskers, and then watched as the backwash frothed back into the bottle. He tried handing me the bottle; I pretended not to see. Still, he insisted, tapping it against my arm until I could not ignore it. In the end, I surrendered. I had already taken one hospital pass. I could take another. In for a penny, in for a pound.

Yet as I took the smallest possible sip of ice coffee that was possible – smaller than any measly sip of communion wine that I have ever been offered – I realised, perhaps for the first time in my life, how Jesus could be fully present in a meal. It was, as a friend of mine once put it, one of life's 'thin moments', when the gap between this life and the next was little more than a thin film, with heaven breaking through to earth. Strangers made friends over a meal in the name of Jesus.

The adventure took me to new territory. Firstly, a new physical territory. I sat in a new place, with a new person and ate a new meal. But then it also took me to new spiritual territory. It opened me up to beliefs, realities and experiences that enlarged my picture of God's reign on earth as it is in heaven.

When we read the Story of the Adventure, we see Jesus' apprentice-followers being taken into new territory. It is confronting: they are sitting on foreign ground, eating dirty food and backwashed drink, touching things that are unclean to them. The muscles of their souls are stretching and, like a muscle that is stretched, there is discomfort, even pain.

After sharing in the miracle of the feeding, there is more stretching than ever for Jesus' disciples. They are questioned by the authorities about their eating habits. They watch as their rabbi, too, is forced to enlarge his mission to include a woman outside of the family of Israel. After her, others are healed who are not of the Jewish race either. They again cross the Sea of Galilee and participate in another feeding miracle, but this time on the Gentile side of the lake. The adventure has taken them into frighteningly new territory.

Then, in their discomfort, they are stretched into a new spiritual territory. They are open to a new wisdom and understanding that they would not have seen if they had not been stretched. They begin to see the world from the point of view of the lost or marginalised and they wonder whether the God of Abraham might also be the God of the Outcast, too. They begin to compare the positional power of the rulers to the generous authority of Jesus and they start to wonder who they would prefer to be king.

Finally, it is Jesus himself who asks the question. The question that the rulers have asked, that the crowds – both Jewish and Gentile – have asked. The question that even the disciples have asked as the storm on the lake was silenced by Jesus around them.

'Who am I?'

And, having followed their rabbi into new spiritual territory, the apprentices now had an answer.

The way today: do something!

The Way of the Adventure operates against the backdrop of Jesus having more faith in his disciples than his disciples have in him. The apprenticeship, therefore, is not a learn-and-repeat way of learning. Rather, Jesus shows the ropes but then hands them over. He asks us to perform miracles. He leads us into new territory. In doing so, we discover things about him and about ourselves that we wouldn't have believed

So, how might this story be written in our lives?

A number of years ago, I started a formal mentoring relationship with a young man that I knew. He was (at the time) a university student and a youth leader at his church. I was a few years older than him. Once we had cleared up that I didn't have any great wisdom or secret insights to offer, but that I would be able to offer an honest, genuine relationship, we were ready to begin.

But what to do? What do a mentor and a mentee (I've never found a good version of this word) do together?

As it happened, our questions got answered in a fortuitous coincidence. Because of our different schedules, the best time for us to meet was early on a Wednesday morning. At the same time, the chaplain at the local state high school was running a breakfast club and needed volunteers. So, the two of us would meet at the high school and spend forty-five minutes making toast for the seemingly bottomless stomachs of the young people who came rabbling through the door. Then, we would go and have breakfast ourselves and chat about whatever was going on in our lives and our apprenticeship to follow Jesus.

Still, it was probably the first half of the meeting that was most meaningful. It was there we got to have an adventure together. As anyone who works with adolescents knows, it is indeed new territory. Hearing the foreign babble of teenagers and their strange music and customs, you could not help but think we were like missionaries in a foreign land.

But it was this that gave us the opportunity to serve and grow, and to learn a little about ourselves, others and God.

So ... if you choose to live the Story of the Call by supporting others as they grow as apprentice-followers of Jesus, and if you take the time to grow an organic relationship through the tried and true method of eating a sack of salt with someone, then I urge you – with all the persuasion that I can pour into the words you are reading – I urge you to:

Do something.

Volunteer at a breakfast club. Tutor some newly arrived refugees. Knit blankets for the homeless. Mow the lawns of elderly neighbours. Go for a walk in a park and pick up rubbish. Read the newspaper and pray together about what you read. Write letters to politicians. Write cards for people who are sick. Visit different religious buildings around your city (including secular temples of shopping centres and sporting fields). Walk through a cemetery. Make art together. Learn magic tricks and do them in children's hospitals. Paint a fence. Wash a plate.

It doesn't particularly matter what you do. But do something. Cross the lake – find new territory. Go to the edge of what you know then take one step further. Move until you feel your spirit stretch. Don't just sit and talk and read books and do courses. Don't just fill your already over-educated head with more data. If you sit and eat but don't exercise, you will become obese. The same is true of discipleship.

It you are reading this, wondering what to do and quickly compiling a list of things you can't do or don't have, then I invite you to remember the story of Jesus sharing a miracle. If you find it hard to think of what to do, ask the one-and-only question you ever need to ask: What have I been given? Take it, give thanks and share it. Watch it multiply. Let it take you to new places and look forward to meeting Jesus there.

The way today: action first, words later

Tell me, I'll forget.
Show me, I'll remember.
Involve me, I will understand.

—Chinese proverb

Take a piece of paper. It can be a sticky note, an A4 sheet or a piece of newspaper – amazingly, the size doesn't matter. Then I want you to fold it in half ten times. Go ahead – do it! The next paragraph will still be here when you get back. But don't cheat.

(Seriously, don't cheat! Only read on if you've given it a go.)

What did you find? Could you get to ten? Conventional wisdom would say that you would have reached a maximum of seven folds.[5]

So, what if I had just told you that? Would you have believed me? Possibly. Why would I lie about something like that? But then again, without doing it, seven does seem like a very small number …

I was once at a cafe with my sister and a flatmate when we overheard an eager young boy talking to his parents at the table next to us. 'When we get home,' he said, with the breathless enthusiasm that is a pleasure reserved for the young, 'we have to do this! We need to get a bowl of water, sprinkle pepper all over the top, and then add a drop of dishwashing detergent onto the middle'. His parents were curious. 'What will happen?' they asked. By this stage we were all unashamedly leaning in to hear the answer. 'You'll see!' was all the boy replied.

Needless to say, as soon as we were home, we rushed to try the experiment ourselves. (If you want to put the book down and do this yourself, that's okay – I fully understand how you feel and won't be offended!)

---

[5] There is actually some very creative science that calculates what length and thickness a piece of paper needs to be to be able to fold more times. Most notably, a high school student named Britney Gallivan actually has folded a piece of paper 12 times.

One of the great themes through Mark's Story of Discipleship is the theme of mystery. From the start, we, the readers, have a secret knowledge that no one else knows. Jesus doesn't give away the answer before he has asked the question. His whole approach is like the boy in the cafe. He communicates in secrets and in signs. Amazingly, even when people (or spiritual forces) seem to get his message, Jesus tells them to keep quiet and tell no one.

He instead invites his disciples to act first, then work out the belief later.

Once again, our usual experience of discipleship works the other way. Normally, we try to teach new thinking, hoping that it will lead to new action. We constantly give people the answer as quickly and as pre-packaged as possible. It is the spiritual equivalent of fast food. Mass produced. Time efficient. Addictively tasty. In my ministry, I have spent more time in this zone than I would like.

However, Jesus' way was different. He made people gather their own ingredients and make their own meals. Instead of trying to get his disciples to *think* their way into a new way of acting, he encourages them to *act* their way into a new way of thinking.[6] He takes his disciples into new territory and lets them see for themselves.

There are numerous ways that this approach could enrich our faith communities, but perhaps the most remarkable thing about the Way of the Rabbi is that it enables us to disciple those who do not yet know Jesus.

The embodiment of this story is beautifully captured in one of the stories of the community builder, Dave Andrews, who tells the story of his interactions with an illegal community of squatters in India.[7] With no work, no money and no land, these people were forced to live in slums or, more likely, to squat on public land. This, of course, led them

---

6 Michael Frost & Alan Hirsch, *The Shaping of Things to Come* (Peabody: Hendrickson, 2003).

7 Dave Andrews, *Compassionate Community Work* (Carlisle: Piquant, 2006), 214–218.

into all sorts of problems with the law and the police were an ever-present threat.

Andrews and his colleagues spent long hours discussing the problems of this vulnerable group and possible solutions. To begin with, there was a powerful urge from the community to respond to the police with violence. However, through collaboration and the input of Andrews, the community eventually came to the remarkable consensus of inviting the police to share tea with them.

The meeting was organised and sure enough the police turned up. While there was much tension, this remarkable, merciful move resulted in a truce in the cycle of violence. Each side could share their needs and the binds that they were in. Yet in doing that, they negotiated a way to meet the needs of both groups.

From that event, Andrews was able to point the community back to the words of Rabbi Jesus (though, of course, they called him Guru): if your enemy is thirsty, give them something to drink. Now convinced of the power of the way of Jesus, the community began to use the words of Jesus as a reference point for solving other problems in the future. In other words, Jesus became the central figure in how this group was saved from the powers that dehumanised and destroyed their lives. They had acted their way into a new way of believing.

And so here in the adventure we find a single self-evident truth, a truth that can, and even must, guide us in this time and place: you can't find new seas until you can't see the shore.

May this generation, like so many before it, see the faithful God and the fearful followers timidly step into new territory together.

Finding our way: The fifth and sixth questions

Like the Stories of the Call and the Relationship, the Story of the Adventure leaves us with questions to ask of ourselves day after day and year after year. The questions of this story inspire us to consider the faith that Jesus has in us and how he is inviting us to participate actively (rather than passively) in our apprenticeship and the learning that comes from it.

What have I been given?

This question moves our mind from our doubts and fears in order to invite us to see the creative possibilities that emerge from the gifts of God. Implicit in this question is the idea that, when we discover what we have been given, we will go and share it. This step inevitably takes us into new territory, and this disequilibrium in our lives awakens us from routines and catalyses change.

What have I been learning?

Jesus' Way does not require answers at its outset. The Story of the Adventure sees Jesus inviting questions through the way he lives his life and letting his disciples find the answers through their experiences. Given the active nature of our apprenticeship, we do well to regularly stop to reflect what we have been learning through all of it. Through asking this question, we can put words on our experiences and take our new way of being into the future.

The Story of the Way

Mark 8:31–10:52

Featuring ...

Backdrop: the turning point

Those who died along the Way

Those who rose along the Way

The trade we are apprenticed to

The way today: ways of dying

The way today: ways of rising

Finding our way: the seventh and eighth questions

Backdrop: the turning point

Mark 8:31–38

*When Christ calls a man,
he bids him come and die.*

—Dietrich Bonhoeffer[1]

Do you remember the first time you saw *The Wizard of Oz*? (If you haven't seen it, perhaps you should, because I'm about to spoil it.) Do you remember the sense of crisis as Dorothy was torn from her own world with no one to protect her but her basket-sized puppy? The way she confronted the new world of new creatures and new rules?

Do you remember the sense of danger as the Wicked Witch of the West cackled her threats? Or the equally powerful sense of hope in discovering the existence of the great, powerful and wonderful Wizard of Oz? The sense of purpose as Dorothy strode down the Yellow Brick Road, the path of salvation to the Emerald City? Do you remember the terror of the dangers she faced? The curious relief of the allies she formed? The sense of victory as she overcame each and every obstacle to reach her goal?

And do you remember the moment of sheer disappointment when you discovered that the great and powerful Wizard was little more than a man behind a curtain?

We connect with this moment because deep down we know that the shining light of hope has a dark ring around its edge. There is no way around it: hope is a risk. When our hopes are not realised, it crushes us. There are few sadder sights in life than seeing someone betrayed by hope so severely or so often that they give up hope altogether. Still, if our lives prove to be a nightmare, we learn it is dangerous to dream. We discover that the wizard is nothing more than a man – a good man, yes, but a bad

---

1 Dietrich Bonhoeffer, *The Cost of Discipleship* (New York: Simon & Schuster, 1959), 89.

wizard. We know this feeling. It happens at the end of a long journey with illness and the magic abilities of the doctor evaporate as she says, 'There is nothing more we can do'. It happens when a trusted friend betrays a confidence or fails to come through when the chips are down.

It happens when our religious leaders turn out to not be what we thought they would be.

Our last chapter of the Story of Discipleship ended with Peter recognising something of who Jesus was: that he was the Mashiach, the Messiah, the Christ, the Anointed. Given everything we associate with the word 'Christ' (particularly as Jesus' 'surname'), we need to remember that for Peter, this almost certainly did not mean that he thought of Jesus as 'divine', and certainly not as the 'incarnate second person of the Trinity'. But that word Mashiach did have meaning.

While there are shelves of books written on the different expectations of what the Mashiach would be, in general the following themes can be drawn out:

- God's anointed prophet-king would rise to leadership among the people of Israel.
- This person would then restore Israel to her purpose, fulfilling the promises God had made to his people. These promises included being a special, set apart nation; a people blessed by God, and a people who would be great among the other nations.
- This would most likely need to occur by overcoming those who oppressed Israel (i.e. the Empire of Rome) and by restoring Israel's religion in the Temple, the law and purity.

The Jewish people looked back into their stories for someone like this and they found people like Moses and David. Naturally they imagined that the Mashiach would look similar.

So, when Peter says the words, 'You are the Mashiach', he has this picture in the back of his head. He has seen enough of Jesus to make him believe that Jesus could be a prophet like Moses or a king like David.

However, for Jesus, this is where everything must change. With his identity as God's anointed person recognised, he must now teach them exactly what that means. So, at this point, which corresponds to the nearly exactly halfway point of the book, the story hinges with these words:

'He then began to teach them that the Son of Man must
suffer
be rejected
be killed
and rise.'

This is the turning point of the story. The disciples have discovered that Jesus is the Messiah. Now they have to discover what kind of Messiah Jesus will be. The question is hardly just academic; it is deeply personal. They are his 12. They bathe in his dust wherever he walks. They are his apprentices, destined to take over his work. His life is a blueprint for theirs. But what did he just say his life will be?

Try to imagine the sudden drop of fear. They thought they were following a wizard but now they realise he is just a man. A good man, but a bad wizard. A man whose blood could drip just like theirs; whose nerves could feel, just like theirs. A man who will weep when he is rejected, scream when he is nailed and groan as he dies.

So, with a rush of blood to the head, Peter rebukes Jesus. He tells him straight. But Jesus rebukes Peter back. I can't imagine what it is like to be rebuked by Jesus but given that elsewhere when he rebuked, storms stopped and demons fled, I can't imagine it would be gentle.

So, with that rebuke, the story hinges again. Not the Story of Jesus but the Story of Discipleship. Our story. We have recognised the Messiah but now we are learning what kind of Messiah he will be. In the same way, we have recognised and followed the call. Now we have to learn what kind of call it will be.

The call was simple: *'Follow me.'*

Now Jesus adds something.

'If anyone wants to follow after me, they must
deny themselves
take up their cross
and follow me.'

Then, with the determination of Dorothy, he turns on his heels and begins to walk down the road. Just over sixty miles ahead lies the destiny he has just foretold. Those who were to be his disciples follow him towards Jerusalem. Or, as Mark calls it over half-a-dozen times, they follow him along the Way.

Those who died along the Way

Mark 9:33–37
Mark 10:17–31
Mark 10:35–45

So, what happens along the Way? Well, first and foremost, things die.

At the beginning of the journey, there is an argument between the disciples on the Way to Capernaum. It is a classic schoolyard argument. Do you remember these arguments about the social standing of every person? Who is better than who at what? Who is the fastest runner? Who is the best at maths? Who is the funniest? Who is the prettiest? Who is the richest? Who would you pick first if you were captain of a team? Who's your *best* friend?

Jesus sees this and asks, 'What were you arguing about?'

All we know is that the disciples were arguing about who was the *greatest*. The greatest at what? We are not told. What we are told is that they were embarrassed about it. They had made sure that the argument was out of earshot of their rabbi and when they realise that he had noticed, they adopt the mute persona of a guilty, sprung child.

Jesus sits down. In other words, he adopts the authoritative posture of a rabbi. With a single sentence, he puts to death their spirit of ambition. This kingdom is not run by the alphas or those who rule the roost of the schoolyard. It belongs to the servants. The little ones. The last, the least and the lost.

The idol called 'Greatness' must be cast down. It must die.

At the end of the journey, the Way begins to rise. It is an uphill walk. They are beginning their ascent up Zion, to Jerusalem. The two brothers in the 12 – James and John – know that this is their time to ask. It is now or never. The iron is hot, so they strike.

'We want you to do what we ask of you.'

'What do you want me to do for you?' the rabbi replies.

'When you arrive in your glory, we want to sit next to you, one on your right and the other on your left.'

What has led to this request? When had they first talked about this? Was it the night that Jesus had called them from their fishing boats? Or when they had begun to see the signs he performed? Or perhaps on the mountain where Jesus was transfigured, where Moses and Elijah stood either side of him?

Jesus sees that something has to die. He tells the brothers (and the rest of the 12, once they hear about it) that they do not know what they are asking.

For, at the end of the Way, Jesus will indeed be lifted up and proclaimed the King of the Jews. And there, beside him, will be those whose place was prepared. One on his right and the other on his left.

'What are you arguing about? What do you want me to do for you?' The rabbi's questions have a way of cutting down into the core of what is wrong with his disciples. These are questions that can still pierce us, even today. What do you argue about? What do you want done for you? What motives are behind these things?

In between these two stories, there was a death along the Way that surpassed them all. As Jesus is walking, a man runs up to him, his long robes hoisted in his hands so that he will not trip. He crashes to his knees in front of Jesus, the stones on the road cutting first his clothes and then his skin. He begs Jesus to reveal to him what he needs to do to be part of the new age that Jesus is beginning.

Rabbi Jesus sees that this man wants to be a disciple. 'Well, what does the law command you?' The man admits no guilt and Jesus accepts that. In fact, looking on him, Jesus loves him. He wants him to be a disciple. He is going to invite him, to issue him the call. But …

… something has to die. Yes, Jesus loves him. But he loves him in the same way that many mothers love their children: just the way we are, but enough to not leave us that way. Jesus knows exactly what needs to be killed. Greed. Selfishness. Security. Again, it only takes one sentence to pass the sentence. But that one sentence is enough to make the man's face sag in sorrow. Enough to get the man to push his knuckles into the ground and rise up to his feet. Enough to make him turn on his heels and walk back through the crowd that had just witnessed his earnest zeal. Enough to make him grieve.

It is here that you and I must look at each other honestly. Not as author and reader, but as human and human walking the Way together. We must admit to one another that there are things within us that must die.

Ambition, greed, glory, lust, pride, bitterness, jealousy, hatred, ingratitude – whatever it is.

I don't need to tell you what yours is and you can't tell me what mine is.

Yet perhaps by admitting this together, we might have the courage to face the rabbi and allow him to speak a sentence into our life. A sentence that might put something to death.

Those who rose along the Way

Mark 9:14–32
Mark 10:13–16
Mark 10:46–52

'What are you arguing about?'

'What do you want me to do for you?'

Along the Way, we have heard each of these questions, each time leading to the death of something in the lives of those to whom Jesus asked the questions. But we will hear each of these questions again.

'What are you arguing about?'

Conflict always turns heads and this one was a big one. The disciples of Rabbi Jesus, other rabbis of the law, and a large crowd, have gathered. It is not clear what was going on.

When Jesus asks the question, a man steps forward. His son is unwell. Possessed, so it seems. He has sought Jesus' apprentice-followers but even they cannot help. Things are starting to spiral out of control. Fear has set in. The doctors can't help. The teachers have no answers. Now even a miracle seems out of the question.

After years of disappointment, the father has given up on hope. He believes, yet he cannot believe. His heart can't bear the pain of total hope, total trust. Not after everything.

That is enough for Jesus. At the bottom of the pit, with a doubting father and a convulsing son in front of him, he speaks his command. For a moment, things stop. Silence. Stillness. Death?

Then, Jesus touches the boy's hand and
raises
him
up.

'What do you want me to do for you?'

In Jericho there was a blind man named Bartimaeus, which simply means the 'son of Timaeus'. Of course, Bartimaeus could not read, he did not have a trade and he would never be a desirable husband for anyone's daughter. He was a beggar.

He knows that Jesus is passing through but he does not know where. He can hear the crowd, feel the buzz and smell the dust in the air as the people gather. But which one is Jesus? To that question, as with so much of his life, he is literally in the dark.

So, he shouts. It's like throwing all your darts at the board at once. One is bound to hit. The son of Timaeus screams out for the son of David. He begs, not for alms but for mercy.

Jesus, the master of compassion, does exactly what most of us do not do when we come across a beggar. He stops. And he calls the son of Timaeus to him. With that call, he *raises him up.*

Timaeus' son leaps to his feet and comes to Jesus.

'What do you want me to do for you?'

This time, it is not ambition, glory or honour that he seeks. While the sons of Zebedee, James and John, want to stand where Moses and Elijah stood, the son of Timaeus just wants to see. With a word from Jesus, he receives his request and, immediately, he begins to follow Jesus along the Way.

Then, in the middle of these two stories – the meat in the Markan sandwich – is the story of the little ones.

Some cultures, like mine, are beauty cultures. Other cultures, like Jesus', are wisdom cultures. In beauty cultures, pleasure and aesthetics are prized and so youth is a commodity. In wisdom cultures, the currency is in morality, experience and storytelling, and so age is an advantage.

Most of us are in a beauty culture. We lie about our age to make ourselves younger (something that would never happen in a wisdom culture). The family is centred on the children. We think endlessly about children's rights but could go a year without talking about elder abuse.

This is why we might find it difficult to understand why the disciples would send the children away. Given how much time our churches today spend agonising over children's ministries, it seems strange that the disciples don't share this value.

This is also the reason why we miss the seismic impact that Jesus' words would have had. He takes these children – seen as ignorant and immoral, not cute and innocent as the perception is today – and he blesses them as the paradigm for the new kingdom. And, in doing so, he

raises

them

up.

All along the Way, people try to stop the outsiders from getting to Jesus. The disciples tell those not from their group to stop healing in Jesus' name. The crowd tries to stop the blind son of Timaeus from calling out for mercy. The disciples try to stop the little ones from being brought to Jesus' knee.

Each time, Jesus thwarts the efforts of the boundary keepers. He raises up the little ones, not just from their affliction, but also to the status of disciple, an apprentice of the Christ. There is no one so weak, no one so ill, no one so excluded, no one so little or no one too much a nobody that Jesus won't accept them as a follower on the Way.

The trade we are apprenticed to

Mark 8:31
Mark 9:31
Mark 10:32–34

"Then he began to teach them that the Son of Man must undergo great suffering, and be rejected by the elders, the chief priests, and the scribes, and be killed, and after three days rise again."…

"He was teaching his disciples, saying to them, 'The Son of Man is to be betrayed into human hands, and they will kill him, and three days after being killed, he will rise again."

And again…

"He took the 12 aside again and began to tell them what was to happen to him, saying, 'See, we are going up to Jerusalem, and the Son of Man will be handed over to the chief priests and the scribes, and they will condemn him to death; then they will hand him over to the Gentiles; they will mock him, and spit upon him, and flog him, and kill him, and after three days he will rise again."

Three times along the Way – before they start their journey, in the middle, and as they begin their final climb up the road to Jerusalem – Jesus stops, takes the 12 into a private place and reveals to his apprentice-followers where the Way is leading.

It puts the requests of the disciples, the rich young man, and the sons of Zebedee, into perspective. If you think the Way is a pathway to being the 'greatest' without service, you are wrong. If you think the Way is leading to eternal life without sacrifice, you are wrong. If you think that the Way will lead to glory without pain, you are wrong.

In the secret, quiet and private times – away from the crowd – Jesus makes it clear to his apprentices where their road will end: Death and Resurrection.

Transformative suffering. Radical renewal. Death and Resurrection.

This is the Way of this Rabbi. As they embark on this journey, Jesus makes it clear that the future apprentice-followers will walk this path too.

This is the meaning of the Way: the journey that Jesus takes is the journey that we, his apprentices, must take. This is the trade we are learning from the master.

Transformative suffering. Radical renewal. There are things in us that need to die and things that must be raised up to life.

Day by day we are dying. And we are rising. It is as elemental to the disciple as breathing is to the body. With each breath out, we expel the waste that the body does not need. With each breath in, we renew the life with in us.

Perhaps my favourite sentence in the whole of this story is the way Mark describes the mood of the disciples as the road begins to ascend towards Jerusalem:

"They were on the road, going up to Jerusalem, and Jesus was walking ahead of them; they were amazed, and those who followed were afraid."

As you take to heart the call of Jesus, and seriously consider following him on the Way, no doubt you will soon feel two things: amazed and afraid.

And as those feelings challenge and stir you, consider praying the most honest of prayers, the prayer of the amazed-yet-afraid: 'Lord I believe! Help me in my unbelief!'

The way today: ways of dying

Whatever is to give light must endure burning.

- Victor Frankl

It is said that in our day and age, there is a lie so common that it is told by nearly everyone in the developed world, namely the lie of, 'I have read the terms and conditions'.

That said, I personally think there is another lie that might not be quite as frequently told, but which is nonetheless far more damaging. For me, the most insidious lie that is believed in the modern world is, 'I can make all your pain go away and make all your dreams come true.'[2]

This is the lie that has been told of virtually every product and service that you have purchased. Of course, it takes many forms:

'Smell this way and you'll never get rejected for sex again.'

'Drink this and become the life of the party.'

'Buy this car and finally be free.'

'Cook this meal and your family will stop fighting.'

'Vote for me and enjoy the prosperity.'

'Get this insurance and you will be safe.'

Et cetera, et cetera, et cetera. In some form or another, every product makes a promise it cannot truly keep. Of course, some are more noble causes, yet they use the same syntax:

'Eat your vegetables and you'll never get cancer.'

'Wear your seatbelt and you won't die.'

'Donate now and lives will be saved.'

Noble, yes, but still lies. Of course, where it most stings is when the same marketing is used for spiritual purposes:

---

2 Clive Hamilton, *Affluenza* (Crows Nest: Allen & Unwin, 2005).

'Trust in God and you will never be poor.'

'Pray to Jesus and it will all be okay.'

'Have faith and you will have nothing to fear.'

In the world of plastic promises, it is my greatest regret that we, as God's people, have been so cowardly. We should feel ashamed. We should stand up and apologise to the world for selling it a product when we were meant to have been giving it a gift. We should thank them for not attending our churches as a protest to our lies. We should beg for forgiveness for ever using Jesus' name to propagate the lie, 'I can make all your pain go away and make all your dreams come true'.

I raise such a protest to this false-promise for the single reason that our rabbi, Jesus Christ, *makes no such promise.*

The only reason we have chosen to use this worldly, deceptive wording is because we are afraid. We are afraid that our Christian voice won't compete with all the other voices making this promise and that we would then become irrelevant. Well, we have become irrelevant. We are irrelevant because we have been caught out in our lie. The season is here for us to be courageous, not afraid. We must trust that the world's idols will be shown to be false. We must trust in the Way of the Rabbi.

What is that way? First and foremost, it is a way of dying. Yes, as his disciples, Jesus invites us to walk a path of dying. Not to be saved from death but to be saved through death. We do not and cannot escape the inevitable suffering of life.

If we cannot make all the pain go away, what does the Way of the Rabbi have to offer? One of my dear mentors introduced me to a piece of old wisdom from an anonymous source: suffering is not a question that can be answered, or a problem that can be solved; instead, it is a mystery that demands a presence.

It is this *presence* that promises to be transformative. In dwelling on the life of Jesus, the followers of the Way were captivated by a new idea, namely that loss and pain were no longer the abandonment of

God, but rather that God could be *present*, even in the worst of life. No longer do we go to that dark place alone.

The early followers of the Way explored how this presence transforms suffering in two distinct ways. Firstly, those of us who follow the Way of Jesus *are transformed through suffering*. Consider the work of a gardener. A gardener is not able to make a seed grow into a flourishing plant. All she is able to do is create conditions that may support that growth. Part of doing that is to pull out anything that may be an obstacle to growth; rocks and weeds, roots and clay, hardness and waste. Even dead branches must be pruned. It all has to be pulled out before the gardener begins and it has to be kept out as she goes. Suffering is the gardening of our growth.

Throughout the history of Christianity there have been spiritual practices of pulling out and putting to death everything that stops our growth.

The season of Lent (the forty days before Easter), while now little more than a slightly spiritualised version of New Year's resolutions, was designed to set aside a time of the year to cleanse your life of problematic issues. The Ignatian practice of Examen was a daily process of reflection on where God had been present in your day and where you had strayed from God's presence. The longstanding practice of confession was designed to force us to reflect honestly on our conduct and where we needed God's transformative grace in the midst of it. In modern times, Life Transformation Groups have regenerated this practice under the framework of accountability within a supportive, trusting relationship.

Jean Varnier, founder of L'Arche, defines health as learning to live with our brokenness.[3] Reading through the New Testament, it is impossible to miss that the earliest disciples of Jesus were able to see suffering as a possibility for transformation. Paul wrote of discovering

---

3 Stanley Hauerwas and Jean Varnier, *Living Gently in a Violent World* (Downers Grove: IVP, 2008).

that Christ's 'power is made perfect in weakness', Peter saw his griefs as a purifying fire, and James celebrated trials as the classroom of learning virtues such as perseverance, maturity and wisdom.[4]

The second way of transformative suffering is to *transform the very nature of suffering*. One of the most difficult tasks of the early disciples was to reconcile the idea of a good man (Jesus) suffering such a ghastly death. The very concept challenged their notion of suffering as a punishment for evil. But when they searched their Scriptures for examples of a good person suffering, they found notions such as the following in Isaiah: "He has borne our infirmities and carried our diseases ... he was wounded for our transgressions ... upon him was the punishment that made us whole, and by his bruises we are healed'.[5]

This opened a new door to the understanding of suffering, namely that one person's suffering may be for the betterment of another. Hence, the first missionaries began to see their trials and weaknesses as opportunities to bring their message to others. Just as Jesus' ministry involved suffering to bring salvation, his apprentices began to see their suffering as a way of bringing peace to others. Indeed, this revolution of perspective was so profound, that suffering was welcomed (rather than resisted) as a transformative experience that produces the depth needed to comfort the suffering of others.[6]

Doubtlessly, at some time in your life you would have been inspired by a story of a person who transformed their pain into a gift to the world. The first time that I personally witnessed this with my own eyes was when I met a man named Paul Stanley in June 2012. He had come, at my invitation, to deliver a short presentation to students of the school where I was working as a counsellor. Given the size of the school, he had agreed to do a series of presentations, one for each year level.

---

[4] 2 Corinthians 12:2–10; 1 Peter 1:6–7; James 1:2–5.
[5] Isaiah 53:4–5.
[6] 2 Corinthians 1:3–7.

I sat next to him while the students filed in. Out of the corner of my eye, I could see him mentally preparing what he was about to say. He was like an old warrior: fixed gaze, clenched jaw, steeled concentration. When the students were seated, I stood up and introduced him. Just before he rose to begin his presentation, he took one long, deep, laboured breath.

With the microphone in hand, Paul then spoke with the sincerest honesty I think I have ever witnessed. He told the story of an event in September 2006, when his fifteen-year-old son Matthew went to a party with other people his age. As Matthew was leaving with friends, another young man, who had been drinking heavily and apparently causing trouble, challenged Matthew and his friends. When Matthew tried to pass him, this other boy unleashed a brutal attack of violence that lasted less than two minutes. Paul detailed it all – the attack, the injuries, when he was told of what happened on the phone, when he sat next to his son in hospital, and the moment that Matthew died.

The whole presentation was raw – the facts, the emotion, the grief, the passion, the love. As raw as meat in the mincer.

Then, an hour later, Paul gave the same presentation, preceded by the same long, deep, laboured breath. He told the story four times that day.

That is what Paul does. He speaks. He writes. He tours. He campaigns. Every day he pushes with the pain, not against it, to tell his story and to try to save families from experiencing what he did.[7] His mission does not take away his suffering, but it does transform it.

Of course, this chapter cannot be the final words on the mystery of suffering. To speak or write about such a difficult topic inevitably risks turning a profound, unique experience into nothing more than an intellectual puzzle. Like any mystery, perhaps the more appropriate response is silence.

---

[7] You can look at the transformative work that Paul (and others) are doing at http://www.matthewstanleyfoundation.com.au/.

Still – and I say this for myself – it is a wondrous thing to me that our apprenticeship extends even to these depths of living. In this way, the transformation of suffering is just as mysterious as the phenomenon of suffering. Just as I am at a loss to explain the agony of pain, equally I am lost for words to explain the courage, peace, meaning and hope that people can find within it.

Perhaps you can now see why I am calling this generation of disciples to abandon the empty promises of marketing. The lies of escaping the inevitable suffering of life wane in the light of the Way of Jesus, who can transform suffering and transform us through suffering. If you want to escape suffering, by all means choose another product. But do let me know how it works out for you.

Creating a rhythm of life that transforms suffering will lead you to dance to the beat of a different drum. There are many people throughout history who you can turn to for inspiration. There are probably some in your midst who can show you the way it is done. When you learn to dance to this rhythm, it is amazing how many others begin to tap their toes.

The way today: ways of rising

Imagine you are in hospital with a disease so serious that your life is at risk. The doctor comes into your room with charts, scans and results loaded under her arm. She sits beside your bed and tells you that she is going to have to perform radical surgery. Thankfully, she is too old to be using the word 'radical' in the way you might have heard it in the early 1990s. Instead she is using it in its Latin sense, meaning the 'roots'. In other words, radical surgery involves the removal of everything that is causing the problem. The doctor will go in to excise it all; the tumour, the nodes, the secondaries, any diseased tissue, any damaged blood. It is all going to be cut out at its roots.

Now, imagine that part of your apprenticeship with Jesus involves a similar experience, not radical surgery but radical renewal. Renewal at your roots. Renewal to your core. Restored. Revitalised. Recreated. Reborn.

A friend of mine, who happens to be a high school English teacher as well as a committed disciple, hates the overuse of the prefix 're-' in church circles. He says that it carries a presupposition that things are no good now and need to be returned or restored to some ideal. To him, it implies failure.

In a way, he is right. The presupposition behind all the uses of the 're-' prefix is the story of creation. The first act of God the mother is to birth a new creation into a vital experience. The first thing that is revealed about God in the Bible is that God is a creative force. God is always bringing new things into being. The Word and the Spirit who were there as this world began is present in your world today.

In this way, the resurrection of Jesus out of death is a re-birth of a renewed re-creation. It is about the creative energy of Mother God giving birth to this creation anew. It is about a complete restoration of this world and every life within it. Nothing will be untouched. The renewal will reach right down even to the deepest, thinnest roots of ourselves.

This is the fullest meaning of the resurrection event. From this perspective, resurrection is possibly the most misunderstood reality of the Bible. It is not just a magic trick performed so the gospels had a 'happy ending'. It does not mean the resuscitation or reanimation of a corpse. This is what happened to Lazarus and the boy at Nain, where they were brought back to life, not resurrected.

To be resurrected means to be restored to a new life in which the old body has transformed into a new body that, while recognisable and physical, is utterly renewed and imperishable. That is what happened first to Jesus at Easter and, as the New Testament asserts, this is what will ultimately happen to us at the climax of history.[8]

Jesus' resurrection is the new blueprint, the new paradigm and the new template for human existence.

When Jesus calls his disciples to follow him by taking up his cross, he also calls them to follow him by taking up his resurrection. Just as our apprenticeship has us learning how the master transforms suffering, so, too, it has us learning his trade of radical renewal.

So, what does it mean to walk the way of radical renewal in our lives? Well, let's consider gardening again. As we discussed previously, the first thing that gardeners do is pull things out that will get in the way of growth. But the second (and equally important) thing that gardeners do is put things into soil; moisture, nutrients, fertiliser, seeds, mulch. Something that will feed the roots, nourish the plants and grow the produce.

So, to follow along the Way is to enter into the habit of daily radical renewal, a restorative nourishment of our roots. The apprentice-followers of Jesus were constantly engaging in practices that put them into sync with the resurrective and re-creative Spirit of God.

---

8 1 Corinthians 15.

As with the Ways of dying, there is a long history of practices that seek to promote the radical new life of the resurrection. These practices are the way that Jesus' apprentice-followers get in time with the rhythm of new life. Whenever I have seen people develop these, I have seen radical new life spring up around them.

For an entire year my wife, Melissa, took a photo every day of something for which she was grateful. Through this practice, she learnt to live in time with what God was giving her. Her whole day was transformed – radically renewed – into a search for gifts from God that she could photograph.

The missional community, Small Boat Big Sea, have a practice of each person blessing three other people in a week, whether by a kind word, a small gift, a gentle prayer or any other enriching practice. By doing so, they deliberately reorient their lives to focus on giving, serving and actively being the good news in the lives of multiple people.

Over a cup of coffee a friend of mine, Joel, once asked me one of the most elegant questions I have ever been asked: 'What have you been learning recently?' Joel exemplifies someone who is always seeking to learn. He does not just seek knowledge, he seeks true learning – learning that deepens him, challenges him and revitalises him. So, by seeking learning, he chases the thoughts of God and is perpetually renewed.

As a follower of the Way, I invite you to look for daily practices that will place you in harmony with the creative, renewing and resurrecting power of God. Furthermore, as a disciple-maker, I urge you to encourage others in such a practice.

When I close my eyes, I can imagine walking into your community of faith and overhearing people asking each other questions that uncover the renewing of bodies, minds and souls. Questions like, 'What have you been given that you are grateful for today?', 'What have you been learning?', 'Who have you blessed recently?' and 'Where has God shown up unexpectedly?'

Now wouldn't that be radical?

Finding our way: The seventh and eighth questions

In the same way that the preceding Stories have left us with questions to ponder in our own lives, the Story of the Way again gives us reason to pause and to reflect. The questions in this part of Mark's story surround the twofold nature of Jesus' own purpose, namely transformative suffering and radical renewal. These two elements represent the nature of Jesus' trade and consequently the content of our apprenticeship. We integrate this story through two further questions.

What is being weeded out?

This question prompts us to think about the areas of life where there is dissatisfaction, discomfort or even suffering. We are encouraged to acknowledge the real pain of these parts of our lives and to seek comfort in the fact that this does not mean rejection from God but is rather an expected part of living. Furthermore, we imagine the possibility of Jesus' ability to empathise and be present in these struggles. In doing so we, like the writers of the New Testament, are inspired to re-imagine such times as weeding or pruning for the sake of future growth.

What new sprouts are breaking through?

The Story of the Way dares to consider that this journey will result in creation being renewed right down to its roots. As people swept up in that story, we also consider what new things are being planted in our lives. We search through our days with curious eyes, trying to spy the green shoots of new growth that might be emerging into our experience.

The Story of the Twist

Mark 11:1–16:8

Featuring...

Backdrop: the turn of the king

Those who should get it, don't

Those who do get it, shouldn't

Those who follow, flee

The one who dies, lives

The way today: the crafty bargain of perfection

The way today: the best last sentence

Finding our way: the ninth and tenth questions

Backdrop: the turn of the king

Mark 11:1–25

There is a story floating around about an Australian missionary who had been invited to be a guest preacher at a church. Before the service the enthusiastic pastor was showing the missionary through the recently refurbished building. When they came to the front of the worship area, the missionary's eyes were drawn to the large, ornate and artistic cross hung on the wall as the focal point for the congregation. Of all of the renovations, this was the pastor's favourite.

'How much did that cost?' gasped the missionary.

The pastor answered that they had specially commissioned it for many thousands of dollars.

The guest shook his head and said, 'You got ripped off!'

'Why? What do you mean?' the pastor asked, to which the missionary replied, 'There used to be a time when Christians got their crosses for free'.

I do not think, of course, that this missionary was expressing a distaste for the symbol or meaning of the cross. In fact, so many of the values that have been exemplified in his life – sacrifice, courage, suffering alongside the rejects of society, costly love, divine protest – can be represented by that most simple image of two intersecting lines.

What I believe he was protesting against was what the cross had now come to mean in the religious building of this congregation. The whole view of the cross was distorted. It was pretty. It was expensive. Without realising it, it symbolised wealth, power and achievement. To be a disciple who picks up that type of cross seems a far less challenging thing. In fact, it was so wrong that it demanded a comment. It demanded a protest.

It is such an act of protest that is the backdrop to the last of the Stories of Discipleship. Jesus enters into Jerusalem in a parade. The meaning is clear. It is festival time. It is Passover time. A story of liberation is being told in every Hebrew household in the world. It is the story of God calling a prophet to overcome the Roman Empire and lead his people to the land he promised. And here he is! A prophet mighty in words and deeds! A Son of David, to be sure! For the Romans, it meant a threat. For the leaders, it meant questions. Deep, fearful questions. But for the people who came with Jesus, it meant celebration, and the form that their celebration takes carries deep symbolic meaning.

Two centuries earlier, a similar parade took place. Judas Maccabeus had triumphantly entered Jerusalem after defeating the pagan ruler, Antiochus IV Epiphanes, through a ruthless guerrilla warfare campaign. He had earned his name as the Sledgehammer in battle. As his parade entered the capital, people waved branches and sang hymns. His dynasty had lasted a century.

By welcoming Jesus in this same way, the people were unequivocally asking him to be the king that Judas Maccabeus had been.

Judas' first royal act had been one of national pride: he restored the Temple. He cleansed it, purified it and rededicated it. The festival of Hanukkah (meaning 'dedication') is celebrated to this day to remember this event.

Why was restoring the Temple such a high priority? Virtually everywhere that you find temples, you find that they represent three things. Firstly, they are a dwelling place – a 'house' – for a deity, and therefore a place of utter holiness. Secondly, they are a place of sacrifice where offerings are made to appease or appeal to the deity. Finally, they are seen as a place of pride, defining who is right with the deity and who is excluded. The scene we read shows exactly how the Second Temple of Israel had come to represent exactly these things, from the layering of the architecture to gradually exclude people the further they entered, to the elaborate trading system to change 'worldly' money into 'holy' money, to the herds of 'unblemished' animals appropriate enough to appease the Lord.

As Jesus' parade approaches the Temple, you can hear the volume of the crowd's crescendo. Is Jesus going to be this generation's Sledgehammer, striking Caesar like Judas Maccabeus had struck Antiochus or as Moses had struck Pharaoh? What better place to start than the Temple!

But this parade is about to have a twist. Jesus' action in the Temple is not one of pride but one of protest. Jesus had carefully planned it and thought about it overnight. It was not just volatile anger as it is often represented. Jesus' actions were making a statement of what he thought about what the Temple had become. It was akin to the missionary's comment on the expensive, ornate cross in the church. The message of both actions is the same: you have lost the entire meaning of what this faith is about. Jesus is saying (through his actions) that the time of the Temple and all that it represents – holiness, sacrifice and pride – is coming to an end. Indeed, it is being superseded. The message of the Temple and the mission of Jesus simply could not coexist.

Firstly, consider the Temple as a holy place, a sacred dwelling of God. Whenever such a place exists, there is an unequivocal message that goes with it: you can come to God if you are good enough. To be good enough, you have to belong to the special club. You have to be either unblemished or able to go through a ritual cleansing. You have to say the right words at the right time in the right way.

In contrast, the whole life and message of Jesus is the opposite of all the Temple represents. Jesus shows that God comes to us just the way we are. Therefore, he chooses to enact his protest in the 'court of the Gentiles', the outermost area of the Temple where even the 'unclean' could go, and he cries out for a house of prayer *for all nations*, not just one.

Having protested against the Temple as a place of exclusive holiness, Jesus then enacts the end of the era of sacrifice. Temple sacrifice is intended to bridge the gap between a powerless people and an angry god. It is somewhere between a begging system and an attempt at magic (that is, manipulating the powers of the universe to be on your side).

However, soon there will be a sacrifice so costly that all others will seem worthless. The idea of needing to appease an angry god will be replaced with the experience of being welcomed by a loving father. In this Spirit, Jesus dramatically interrupts the sacrificial system. He defiles (not cleanses) the money and the animals that were being used for sacrifice. Like an industrial strike, he stops people being able to transport their goods through the court. Soon there would be no need for this.

Having demonstrated against the Temple's exclusive holiness and punitive sacrificial system, Jesus moves to denounce it as a source of pride. Again, through history, a nation's temple is a place that you have to protect. Sadly, even in our modern world we know all too well what lengths people go to protect 'sacred' land. The Temple Jesus enters was such a place. It is why the Romans built their Jerusalem fortress right up against its walls. It is why Jesus could say it had become a 'den of revolutionaries'. In this way, Jesus' actions sought to demonstrate that faith was more important than ritual; that with a prayer of the faithful, the whole Temple mountain could be uprooted and tossed into the sea. He shows that no place is sacred enough to justify violence. Indeed, when a human life is taken, even in defence of a temple, perhaps we have sacrificed God's true dwelling for the sake of the idol.

The bread around this sandwich is a strange story of Jesus cursing a fig tree. What Mark is illustrating in this story is the same principle that the Gospel of John records with words: whatever branch does not bear fruit will be cut off. What fruit had the Temple produced? Its holiness had produced fruit of exclusion. Its system of sacrifice had produced legalism. Its pride had turned into violence.

Think of what Jesus came to do! To show us that God *comes to us* just the way we are, to give *grace* and *peace* to all people! Jesus and the Temple were night and day; they could not coexist.

There is no doubt that Jesus was being hailed as the returning King of Israel. But, what no one expected was that there was going to be a twist.

Jesus was going to turn the idea of a king inside out. Jesus was putting a twist on everything that everyone expected when God appeared to establish his kingdom. Along with the other stories, the Story of the Twist is important for us to know as the apprentice-followers of Jesus. Because one day – and sooner rather than later – we will find ourselves in the middle of a kingdom that we probably didn't expect.

Those who should get it, don't

Mark 11:27–13:2

Oscar Wilde once remarked that if you want to tell someone the truth, you better make them laugh, otherwise they will kill you for it. This wisdom has been practised throughout centuries, as creative people have sought to speak the truth to the unjust – but frighteningly powerful – societies in which they dwelt. From Aristophanes' *Lysistrata* and Chaucer's *Canterbury Tales*, through to Mark Twain, Charles Dickens, George Orwell (and Wilde himself) and modern creations such as *South Park* and *The Simpsons*, writers have often hidden barbed truths within what appear to be whimsical comedies. It has often been the work of the jesters to say the things that need to be said beneath the garb of laughter.[1] It is like biting into a cake only to be cut by a razor.

This tradition does not just belong to the literary greats, but also to the much more down to earth storytelling of folktales, fables and parables. These, too, lure us in and lower our defences. They dress themselves up as cake. They establish a pattern with which we become comfortable. The first pig builds his house; the wolf blows it down. The second pig builds his house; the wolf blows it down. It is predictable; we are comfortable. It is only when the story twists that we are surprised to find that this cake is not just a cake. The house built out of bricks stands. We are left thinking, reflecting, questioning. And, if the story is pointed enough, we may even be left bleeding.

Among all those in history who have hidden truths in stories, Jesus must sit at the head of their table. Consider this example: Jesus tells a story standing in the midst of multiple systems of power. At his back is the religious, priestly power of the Temple; to his left is the judicial power of the Royal Stoa where the court of the Sanhedrin would meet;

---

1 Michael Frost, *Jesus the Fool* (Springvale: Urban Neighbours of Hope, 2007).

to his right was the imposing military power of the Roman fortress of Antonia, looking over the entire city.

'A man planted a vineyard.' Jesus goes to pains to describe the efforts of the owner. The man blistered his own hands to establish this fertile place of growth. But then, he hands his creation over when he employs tenants to keep the garden. The tenants, like so many of us do when we are given a gift to look after, begin to confuse stewardship with ownership. So, when the harvest comes and the owner sends servants to collect the fruit, the first servant is beaten and sent back by the tenants. The second servant is struck and humiliated.

The third is executed.

One by one, each servant is hurt or killed until … 'He had one left to send. A son, whom he loved.'

Jesus' crowd hold their breath to hear the twist. Like the owner, they expect a different result. Their thoughts harmonise with those of the owner: 'Surely they will respect the son! Even the tenants recognise him as the true son, the heir'.

However, not only is the status of the owner's son not compelling enough for the tenants to finally obey, it is this very status that threatens their fragile identities. If the son is the heir, then the vineyard isn't really theirs. They don't truly have the authority to run it however they like.

So, they kill the son too. They could not coexist. If this man lived, then their time was over. In the end, the twist ends up being that there isn't a twist. The tenants did to the son just what they did to the servants.

Everyone who had bitten into the cake now tasted blood.

The authorities who challenged Jesus were the ones who were meant to get it. They had been given charge over God's garden, his creation. They had the stories, the law, the memories. They knew it all inside out.

When the Son of God arrives, however, they just do not get it. They are unable to recognise someone anointed with God's authority, first with the baptiser, John, and now with Jesus. They don't get that in their effort to gain nationalistic power against those who had occupied their land, they forgot to pay their dues to their ultimate Lord, whose image they bear.

They don't get that their religious purity has come at the cost of the lives of the vulnerable. They don't get that their religion has emptied the purses of the widows of their very last coins.

They don't get that the sacrifices of the Temple are about to become outdated. They don't get that their efforts to get to God are pointless because God has come to them. They don't get that mercy that goes beyond their law is breaking into their world, like light cracking through the clouds. They don't get that an age is about to come to an end – that not one stone of the world that they had built was going to be left on top of another – neither religious temples nor royal courts nor military fortresses.

It is this image of building that Jesus uses to conclude his parable. In all their efforts to build their own kingdom – a kingdom marked by legal purity, religious exclusion and national ambition – they had created a structure in which Jesus (the true heir of the kingdom) would not fit. There was no space for the stone he represented. So, he became the stone that the builders rejected.

This begs the question for all who seek to follow Jesus, through every age, including me, including you. Does our religion have a place for Jesus? Or, if he showed up, would we find we had no room for him? Would we reject him for our rules, our pride or our ambitions?

And if we are his apprentices might we, too, find ourselves squeezed out by our religion?

Might we have to face that most painful word that Jesus used to describe himself: *rejected*?

Those who do get it, shouldn't

Mark 14:1–9
Mark 15:21
Mark 15:39

First, there is the woman.

Is there any way to truly grasp the significance of whether an X chromosome or a Y chromosome sperm reaches the egg first? That very moment of sheer randomness of whether we will be male or female sets up so much of our experience of life.

There have been plenty of books (though perhaps still not enough) that have detailed what it meant to be a woman in the time of Jesus. For our purposes, we will just summarise all that we need to realise here: this woman was not meant to get it. She did not have the education to get it. She did not have the status to get it. She was not meant to have the common sense to get it.

Yet, with one wordless gesture, she gets it. She is the one who anoints the Anointed One. She is the prophet who anoints the king. She is the priest presiding over the funeral of the Christ. She is scolded for her actions and put back into her place through the patronising lectures of the men. But the rabbi knows that she has got it, and he declares that the Story of Discipleship would never be complete if her story was not told within it.

Then, there is the Roman, a centurion, no less. A man in charge of one hundred men. Battle hardened. Experienced. Leadership material. Good enough at killing to preside over an execution. After all, he had seen enough deaths in his time. What's three more? Just a couple of bandits, and the man charged with calling himself 'King of the Jews'.

Yet the death of this last man is different from all the rest. The way the man cries out, the way that he dies is … different. We do not know what the Roman saw in this revolutionary hanging from the post. But his conclusion was unequivocal: this is the Son of God.

He got it. He got what no one else in the story was able to get. Neither the experts with their books, the crowds with their zeal nor even the disciples had recognised this. Only the voice from heaven and the cries of the demons had acknowledged Jesus as the Son of God so far. This was the secret knowledge that we, as the readers, learnt in the very first sentence of the Book of Mark. But the first time these words are spoken by a human voice, they are said by some who had no right to get it.

The centurion got it. He saw how he died.

In between the stories of the woman and the Roman is the alien – a man from Cyrene, which in modern terms is in the north-east of Libya. Whether he had walked across Egypt or whether he had sailed across the Mediterranean, he was a long way from home.

I have (thankfully) never seen a procession to an execution. I know people who have. I can only imagine the terror of having to carry the means of execution for someone else. It would be like walking to the gallows with the noose around your neck. Yet, this is what Simon of Cyrene is forced to do.

And so the alien becomes the disciple. He literally carries the cross with Jesus. He was not the one who was meant to do this. He was not one of the 12. He had not promised to die with Jesus. He had not been there at the beginning or even on the journey at all until this point. But he was there at the end, in the posture of a disciple.

In the midst of this story, those who truly got it were those who shouldn't have got it. They were outsiders. They were never meant to show this level of devotion, understanding or discipleship.

But who else was there to do it? For those who had followed Jesus had fled.

Those who follow, flee

Mark 14:12–52

In my teenage years, I played a lot of sport. At most sports I was quite mediocre but in Australian football, I had some talent. Therefore, my high school years were punctuated by various trips to represent my town, region or even state in football.

One annual game was between my town and another major regional town about five hundred kilometres away. That year it was my team's turn to travel, so as a team of sixteen-and-seventeen-year-old boys, we climbed into the bus to make the tedious trip down to the game.

The tone of the trip was set at our first stop at a service station. While we were there, some of my teammates stole some pornographic magazines. To pass the time as the bus trundled along the road, people gathered around the magazines, soaking up the images with eyes and mouths wide.

My teammates knew about my faith. Most knew my father was a minister. They knew I sometimes arrived late to Sunday games because of church. I had missed a major representative carnival to attend a youth Bible camp. But beyond what they knew about me, I felt deeply uncomfortable about those magazines. Uncomfortable right in my innards. I did my best not to look but my best wasn't good enough. Turning my head one way at the wrong time, I caught a glimpse. As someone passed the glossy paper around me, I caught a glimpse. As an eager teammate excitedly shared his favourite picture with me, I caught a glimpse.

It was on that bus on an Australian country road, I was first exposed to the power of pornography. But don't get me wrong, I was not an innocent victim. There were things I could have done. I could have shut my eyes. I could have gone to sit up next to the driver. I could have told my teammates how I felt. I could have made a stand. But I didn't.

Standing up is hard. To stand up is to stand out and, contrary to many of our myths of fame, most of us don't want to stand out.

On the journey home came another challenge. To celebrate our win, the coaches bought us minors beer and also rum and cola. Whether it was because of what happened on the journey down or whether it was because I was already known as someone who didn't drink, I didn't drink any of the alcohol even though, as I remember it, all of my teammates were drinking like fish.

Just try to put yourself in my shoes for a moment. Try to remember the pressure of that time of life – the do-or-die instinct to fit in. Try to imagine sitting in that confined space, cold sober, as the noise became louder, as the tongues became looser, as the jokes became coarser.

And then imagine that one of your teammates turns to you – as one of mine did to me – looks at you with slow, unfocused eyes, and slurs the following question: 'When you go to church, do you drink the wine?'

At that stage in my life, I would have liked to think that my faith could withstand torture. But, in that moment, I lied. I denied. I deserted. I looked back at him and said, 'No'. I was seriously scared of standing out. I was scared of what question would come next. I was scared of seeming even weirder than I already was. And for the rest of the trip, I said nothing to anyone because I was afraid.

It was only years later, when I was completing my theological studies, that I found that this was not a new issue for a disciple of Jesus. In the early fourth century, under the Roman Emperor, Diocletian, there was a fresh spate of persecution against the followers of the Way. The edict that was given was to destroy the literature and the property of the Christians. Of course, some brave souls resisted but some succumbed to the pressure. They handed over their books to the emperor's soldiers and so they became known as the *traditores* – the ones who handed over. We still call people traitors in memory of them.

Years later when peace returned, the community of followers faced difficult questions. What do we do about the traitors? Having fallen away so disgracefully, are they still allowed to minister? In particular, are these people still able to baptise or bless the bread and the wine for the Eucharist? Or is their sin too much? Will their failure stop God's miracles from working?

The majority of the time, a group called the Donatists, had a clear answer: the failure of these priests and pastors had invalidated their whole ministry. Any baptism they performed, or any communion they presided over, would not work. The position held for decades.

Some voices, namely the men Cyprian and Augustine, said differently. These men went back to a foundational aspect of the faith: that if it was a matter of worthiness as to who received God's gifts or was able to be part of God's ministry and mission in the world, then none of us would be able to partake in this. As Augustine said, when we perform God's ministry it is holy because of what is done, not because of who does it.[2]

We cannot say for sure, but perhaps part of the story that was in the minds of these leaders were the stories of the disciples at the end of Mark's gospel. Here, those who were following are now fleeing.

Jesus predicts it. At the table of the Passover, usually celebrated with family, Jesus says to his family of apprentices, 'One of you, one of the 12, will betray me'. We know the story well, so it is easy for us to single out Judas, glare at him and wonder what made him do it. Yet Mark does not name Judas here. Instead, we see the disciples, one after the other, asking if it was them he spoke of. The point is that it could have been any of them.

After the meal, Jesus makes the point even more clearly: 'when they strike me, you will flee'. Peter swears an oath but again Jesus puts him in his place. Once again, we often tell of Peter's failure but we then forget Mark clearly states that *all the others said the same*. I can

---

2 An interesting account of what is known as the 'Donatist Controversy' is in Alister E. McGrath, *Christian Theology: An Introduction* (Oxford: Blackwell Publishing, 2001), 478–480.

think of some of the promises that I have prayed or sang to God, and I suppose I have said the same, as well.

Then, in the middle of all this failure, Jesus takes up the bread and the wine, and he shares his sacrifice with these deserting disciples. His faithfulness given to the faithless. His courage given to the fearful – for Judas, for Peter, for the *traditores* and for me, even though under the slightest pressure, I would deny that I even eat such a meal.

It is, as Francis J. Moloney most perfectly said, a broken body for broken people.[3]

---

[3] Francis J. Moloney, *A Body Broken for a Broken People* (Burwood: Collins Dove, 1997).

The one who dies, lives: a disciple's hymn to a crucified rabbi

Mark 15:25-16:4

For many years I worked as a trauma counsellor for refugee survivors of persecution and war. I have heard many stories of the horrors of human violence. I know what it sounds like for a person to put into words the most awful moment of their life: a bomb blast, a gunshot, a beating or even just an ominous knock at the door.

It was these experiences that make me read this part of the gospel differently. Buried underneath two millennia of layers of theology was a real event of human violence.

In particular, I go cold whenever I read this line:

'It was the third hour that they crucified him.'

We all read it every year. We talk and think about it every week; some of us every day. Many of us have seen crosses suspended on churches, imprinted on the front of Bibles, or cast into silver to be hung around our necks. Through the desensitisation that comes from over-exposure, that ghastly sentence has lost its sting.

So, I wonder how these words would have sounded coming from the mouths of those who had witnessed this event. Someone had to have passed this story onto Mark. What did that story sound like when it was told? Were these words choked out between sobs? Were the voices trembling with the fury that only victims of the cruellest injustices can know? Or were the words delivered stoically through gritted teeth, to avoid the potential overwhelming emotion?

The shock of it is clear – it was not meant to end this way. If ever there was a twist in a story, this was it. However, if we think of Chekov's Gun, we can come to see that this wasn't the twist at all. The rabbi knew that living his Way was always going to end up here.

If Jesus' call was to bring the divine into skin-to-skin contact with the destructive forces that had dehumanised God's creation, then at some point he had to touch the most destructive force of all.

If Jesus was to redefine relationships according to the blood of loving covenant rather than the water of family or nation, then at some point he would suffer the fate of those who challenge the cliques of tribalism.

If Jesus' faith in his followers was so great that he could lead them into new spiritual territory, then we could expect that this quest would force us all to explore anew the place of God in the greatest mysteries of our experience – suffering, loneliness and death.

And if Jesus is ultimately walking the Way of transformative suffering and radical renewal, then eventually he would arrive at the place where this path necessarily ends.

In this way, the event of Jesus' death is not the twist. Rather, the greatest twist in this story is that the death of the rabbi isn't the end of discipleship, it is the beginning.

> I sit beneath your humble throne
> A man upon a cross
> Power is not the way this king
> Seeks and saves the lost.
> I gaze upon your humble throne
> The cost of sacrifice
> I gaze upon the only way
> That could lead to life.
> Take but a splinter from your cross
> A thorn that pierced your brow
> And make of these a worthy throne
> And a worthy crown.
> Take my days, take all my days
> And help me follow you
> Even if that means a cross
> Is what I carry too.

The way today: the crafty bargain of perfection

I have a relationship with Perfectionism.

I first met Perfectionism quite early in my life, probably when I was in primary school. The circumstances, as it turns out, were quite common with how others I know have met Perfectionism, in that we first met when we had some success. This came in the form of good marks, recognition from people who mattered to me, and pats on the back for being a 'good boy'. All of this success felt good but it also felt scary. I feared losing it, for I felt that if I lost it, I would lose all this esteem, all this affection. In short, in my child's mind, unless I was perfect, I was worthless.

It was at this point that Perfectionism swaggered into my life like a smug hawker of magic cures. Perfectionism offered me a sleazy deal: 'Obey my ways, and you can maintain your success'. I did not have the critical capabilities to assess this bargain. My worth was on the line, not to mention the affection of the people I needed, so I bought into the deal.

Perfectionism mentored me in his ways: how to fill myself with worry, how to obsess, how to criticise myself, how to agonise over what I could not control, and how to avoid anything that risked failure. To his credit, Perfectionism delivered on his promise. My efforts in his ways were rewarded by more success, more pats on the back, more warm words and more swelling of my ego. His ways got me through secondary school, university and my first jobs.

Like any peddler of snake oil, what he didn't tell me about were the hidden costs and side effects. It was only when I went to work as a counsellor at a large and highly successful private school that I saw how Perfectionism had sold his product, not only with me but with many, many others. It was at this school where I first met students with far more talent than I could dream of, sometimes academically, sometimes physically, sometimes culturally and sometimes in all categories at once. But I also witnessed what their deal with Perfectionism had left them with: a deep sense of fundamental worthlessness, a pervading terror of being shown up as a fraud, a paranoid avoidance of anything that could lead to failure, an inability to enjoy life's natural highs, due to fear of them being taken away, and an abiding sense that the affection of their loved ones was as fragile as the success they had obtained.

Here was Perfectionism's genius, for when they encountered these problems, they immediately turned back to the ways of Perfectionism to get themselves out of it. In other words, they asked for a higher dose, seeking ever higher levels of perfection in order to soothe their insecurities and fears. It was a drug, in all senses of the word. Effective, yet addictive. Powerful, yet destructive.

Make no mistake, Perfectionism is one of the most destructive forces that can enter a human psyche, either individually or collectively.

Likewise, Perfectionism is perhaps the greatest challenge to discipleship. I don't make this statement lightly. I recognise that this perhaps states exactly the opposite of the fundamental way of thinking in our Christian communities at the moment, namely that the greatest challenge to discipleship is sin. But have we actually considered the cost of the deal we have done with perfection in order to overcome our obsession with our sin?

A fine example of what I mean would be the life of Martin Luther. In his youth, Luther became obsessed with sin and so, like me, he did a deal with Perfectionism. Each success urged him to strive harder. Each failure urged him to be more critical, more punishing of himself. Like anyone who lives in fear of being a fraud, his life was filled with terrified effort to avoid being exposed publicly to be as worthless as he felt privately. His spiritual life mirrored this: any expression of love he felt from God was merely for his efforts. Such a life of fear explains why, when he discovered God's message of acceptance of him just as he was – his successes *and* his failures – he then devoted his life to uncompromising critique and rejection of any individual, institution or ideology that forced people to strive for perfection.

When we do a deal for Perfectionism in discipleship, we seriously limit our potential to grow as Jesus' apprentice-followers in a number of ways. Firstly, because of the sheer effort it takes to maintain perfection, we don't allow ourselves to be truly vulnerable and surrender into God's grace. Secondly, our obsession with sin breeds self-criticism and deafens us from believing God's words of acceptance for who we are. Finally, and perhaps most tragically, our fear of failure stops us from beginning so many journeys of discipleship that could lead us to deeper places in our spirituality.

The Story of the Twist teaches us that Jesus' apprentices are never perfect and that failure is neither final nor fatal. It teaches us that perfection is a myth we will not be able to achieve and, as our rabbi, Jesus is willing to pay the cost for our shortfalls. Perhaps an old hymn still has some wisdom for us today:

<blockquote>
Just as I am – without one plea,
But that Thy blood was shed for me
And that Thou bidst me follow Thee –
O Lamb of God, I come, I come!
</blockquote>

The way today: the best last sentence

One of the things that draws me back to the Bible as a story of truth is that every character is depicted authentically. You get people warts 'n' all. No one is an infallible hero.

This extends into the Mark's Story of Discipleship. As we have seen, Jesus' followers are marked by faithlessness, fear and fleeing when times get tough. It seems fitting that the final sentence of the story fits in with this theme. In this sentence, we have the first witnesses to Jesus' empty tomb and their warts 'n' all response:

'They said nothing to anyone, because they were afraid.'

Full stop. The end. Say no more.

Could this be the best last sentence that has ever been written? If not the best, then surely the most honest. There is no airbrushing here. Furthermore, it would have to be the most curious. We are left with more questions than we have answers. How did the story continue? How did the word get out? Knowing the story as the women did, what will we choose to do now?

While many have questioned whether this sentence is a mistake and that the real ending of the gospel is missing, for many others, it is seen as the perfect culmination of Mark's Story of Discipleship. Throughout the story, the Way of the Rabbi isn't one for heroes and it isn't one that just gives the answers. Jesus does not give us a rule book; he gives us a story.

A Story of the Call right where we are, just as we are.

A real, human Story of the Relationship, the type that can only be grown in the time it takes to eat a sack of salt.

A Story of the Adventure that takes us into new territory, first with our bodies and then in our spirits.

A Story of the Way, walking along the path of transformative suffering, pulling the crap out of our lives, and radical renewal, restoring the goodness of creation.

And finally, a Story of the Twist, where the reign of God reverses the expectations of the religions and powers of this world.

To live in this story is exciting, yet it is also threatening. You see, we all like to believe we are in the driver's seat of our own lives. The universe is too frightening otherwise. From the time we realise our infant cries make our carers come for us, we seek to find any control over the world, which to us seems so much more powerful than we can ever be. We need to believe that we have our hands on the wheel, steering our own direction, being in charge of anything that will have an impact on us.

Throughout our lives, we find highly sophisticated ways to feel a sense of safety and power. We develop our knowledge and competence so we can feel capable of handling the challenges life throws at us. We create patterns from our experience to make predictions about the situations we are in or even those we could possibly face. We develop relationships that sustain us, nourish us and protect us. We accumulate resources so we may feel sufficiently stocked, both for the present and the future.

These strategies largely give us the feeling that we are steadily cruising through our life with our hands on the wheel and our feet on the pedals. This is why any experience of loss can be so utterly frightening. Loss has a way of making a mockery of our methods of holding onto control, for none of our knowledge, competence, schema, relationships or possessions are able to save us from loss. What we thought was stone crumbles into sand.

Yet it is not only loss that causes us to give up our illusions of power. Moments of great yet unexpected joy equally leave us shaking our heads at how they could ever have snuck up on us. We stand, full of feeling yet empty of words, knowing that such a gift was beyond our capabilities to produce, beyond our imaginations to predict, beyond our allies to supply and beyond our resources to buy. Such moments of joy happen in spite of our power; in spite of, not because of.

Though at the opposite ends of the human experience, both the moments of great loss and great joy result in the same phenomenon: tears. In grief and joy, our masked countenances crack; we lose control; we weep.

To step onto the Way with the Rabbi of Nazareth will inevitably result in twists you never saw coming. In a way, we shouldn't be surprised, for to become an apprentice-follower means sliding over into the passenger seat and handing over the controls to your Lord God.

I am not long on this journey but already I've had the chance to shed the tears at the twists this road has had for me. I've cried at moments of personal shortfall, where the gospel has confronted me with the cost of my own mistakes. I have cried from compassion, being moved by the Spirit to feel the pain that God feels for the suffering. I have cried from betrayal, as people have taken the kindness I have shown on behalf of Christ and used this vulnerability to hurt me. I have cried when my sense of calling to follow the rabbi has left me rejected by my religion.

Yes, I have cried from loss, yet I have also wept with joy. I have wept to see prayers answered with healing or with peace. I have wept to see many I have loved come to know the Jesus whom I have loved. I have wept in moments when hope has gripped my insides and not let go. I have wept from the healing of both receiving and giving forgiveness. I have wept to see young people I have discipled grow into leaders themselves, doing things far beyond anything I could do. I have wept as the lowly have been lifted up, as wrongs have been righted and as mercy has overcome fear.

Never had I imagined that part of learning how to follow Jesus was learning to weep as Jesus wept. Still, it doesn't matter whether or not I was prepared for it; I wept nonetheless.

So, in the tradition of the Way of the Rabbi and the Story of the Twist, I want to write for you the best last sentence that I can think of. I want to write a sentence that raises more questions than it has answers. A sentence that opens up new stories in your mind, even as you read it. So, to you who are called to live the Way today, I say to you:

Be unprepared.

Finding our way: The ninth and tenth questions

The Story of the Twist turns so many of our assumptions on their heads. We watch how those who should get the message are the ones who get it wrong, while the ones who understand and act most clearly are the ones who were least expected to do just this. Ultimately, this twist is exemplified in the event of Jesus' death: that a moment of supreme horror could possibly be the start of something new and lifegiving. In this way, the Story of the Twist leaves us with two new questions that we probably would never have considered on our own.

Can I be less perfect?

Perfectionism comes with a cost. Its uncompromising nature can leave us without the space to admit weakness, failure or areas for growth. Conversely, when we let go of a need to be perfect, we can find acceptance, and this sense of being good enough provides a freedom to take risks and live life in a way that perfectionism never could.

Am I unprepared?

The desire to be prepared meets a psychological need for a sense of control. An obsession with control, however, can leave us blinkered to other certain experiences in life like surprise, awe, wonder and mystery. Being an apprentice of Jesus means, in part, being open to discovering things and encountering mysteries that are beyond even imagination. Therefore, it is worthwhile to regularly check that our desire for control isn't getting in the way of potential learning and growth that is there to be discovered.

Again, it is the best last sentence that I can think of: be unprepared.

Acknowledgements

If this book is life-giving to you in any way, then it is right to realise that there are many people who helped to make it happen both directly and indirectly. Indirectly, of course I have to acknowledge my parents and family for the teaching and example that helped to form these ideas long before this book was even an idea. For those who taught and mentored my faith (both informally and in official training) and for all those who have been gracious enough to allow me to serve them or serve beside them, your influence on me is infused into every page of this book.

More directly, the formation of this book was shaped by many people. Over the years I received invitations to speak on this topic which gave me the opportunity to prepare but also shape this material. Thanks to early readers (Melissa, Linda, Alwin, Val) for encouragement and feedback, and particularly to the Sparklit Young Australian Christian Writers Award, which gave this book its first exposure to a professional audience. Thanks to Elise for your editorial tidy up which undoubtedly saved me some embarrassment. Finally, I of course must acknowledge Amanda and the team at Morning Star for their will, resourcing, expertise and patience in getting this published.

* 9 7 8 0 6 4 7 5 3 3 4 6 8 *